Noble Morris Design

BUSINESSCARDS

A COLLECTION FROM AROUND THE WORLD

EDITED BY TAKENOBU IGARASHI

BUSINESSCARDS

A COLLECTION FROM AROUND THE WORLD

EDITED BY TAKENOBU IGARASHI

BUSINESSCARDS

世界の名刺

編集＝五十嵐威暢

BUSINESS CARDS
A Collection from around the World

Edited by Takenobu Igarashi © 1989
Published by Graphic-sha Publishing Company Ltd. © 1989

Printed in Japan by Toppan Printing Co., Ltd.

First Edition 1989

Editing and book conception . . . . Takenobu Igarashi
Art direction. . . . . Takenobu Igarashi
Cover design . . . . Takenobu Igarashi
Layout . . . . Kayoko Shiratori
Photography. . . . . T. Nacása & Partners
Preface translations. . . . . Jay W. Thomas
English typesetting . . . . Lynx Inc.
Japanese typesetting. . . . . Sanwa Typesetting Co., Ltd.
Printing and binding. . . . . Toppan Printing Co., Ltd.
Coordinating. . . . . Seiki Okuda

Abbreviations
AD – Art Director
D – Designer
A – Artist
C – Client

The business cards introduced
in this book were chosen solely
for their design.
Unavoidably the information
on a number of cards was not
available at the time of
publication.

本書では，名刺をデザイン作
品としての観点から紹介して
います。
本書に収録した名刺，および
名刺に印刷された情報は，現
在使われていないものも含ん
でいます。

Preface

Business cards are now more interesting than ever before. More than the small, plain rectangles of paper listing a name and address that they used to be, business cards have become an important means of expressing a company, or an individual's identity.

Students and other non-professionals have begun using business cards, not only for identification, but also as a fashionable statement and means of self-expression. The most recent development is a business card with a magnetic strip that enables the holder, through the use of a special phone, to call the company or person without dialing. Consequently, business card design is becoming a lively aspect of the field of graphic design.

This book introduces a number of innovative business cards from all over the word in hopes to stimulate and inspire the designer, as well as to give all readers a comprehensive view of the state of this often neglected art. I received the majority of the cards in this book directly from their respective designers for the specific purpose of reproducing them. There are, however, a number of cards used from my personal collection, whose designers and pertinent information I could not ascertain. I trust that these individuals will understand and give their consent, considering the purpose of this book.

My sincere thanks to those designers who were so willing to have their works appear in this volume of Business Cards: A Collection From Around the World.

                                                    Takenobu Igarashi

はじめに

名刺の世界が面白くなってきた。今日，名刺は単に名前や住所が記された一片の紙きれではない。個人や社会のアイデンティティを主張する重要なメディアとなりつつある。

クレジットカードのように磁気テープに情報を記憶させて，この名刺を使うと，ダイヤルしないで，相手先に電話がかけられる新種の研究も進行中だ。

仕事を持たない家庭の主婦や学生達も名刺を使い始めた。名刺は使う人の身分をあかす手だての機能を超えつつある。持つことがファッションであり，遊びであり，自己主張につながる。名刺のデザインも，したがってにぎやかに活況を呈している。

本書は広く世界から面白い名刺のデザインを紹介している。名刺のデザインをもっと楽しいものにしたいと願う私個人の気持ちが，出版というかたちになった。

収録された名刺の中には，私個人の手元にいつのまにか集まった作者不明のものもある。

必要なデータは可能な限り収集の努力を続けたが，わからずじまいのものも多い。掲載の了解を得る手だてのないものもあったが，出版の意図に免じて許していただきたいと思う。

しかし大半の名刺は出版に際して世界のデザイナー達から送られてきたものである。世界のデザイナーが力を貸してくれて，一冊の本にまとめることができた。

この場を借りてお礼を申し上げたいと思う。

名刺よ，もっと面白くなれ。

五十嵐　威暢

Akagi Design
Design firm
USA 1985
Akagi Design
AD, D · Dough Akagi
デザイン会社

Rudy Vanderlans
Graphic designer
USA 1987
Emigre Graphics
AD, D, A · Rudy Vanderlans
グラフィックデザイナー

Rod Dyer
Graphic designer
USA
Rod Dyer Group Inc.
AD, D · Rod Dyer
グラフィックデザイナー

By Design
Graphic design firm
USA
C · By Design
グラフィックデザイン会社

Nolte European Design
Design group
West Germany 1987
Randolph Nolte Creative Consultants
AD, D · Randolph Nolte
デザイン会社グループ

Dyer/Kahn, Inc.
Graphic design firm
USA
Dyer/Kahn, Inc.
AD · Rod Dyer
グラフィックデザイン会社

Seestrasse 51 CH-8942 Oberrieden Tel 01 721 13 42

Forschung und Beratung für Kommunikationsmanagement
und Medienentwicklung

Publicom AG

René Grossenbacher, lic. phil. I
Geschäftsführer

169 South
Bluff Street
St. George,
Utah 84770
801-628-4265

Bruce J. Roberts
Owner

David Smith
Graphic designer
USA
David Smith
AD, D · David Smith
グラフィックデザイナー

Publicom AG
Switzerland 1986
Gottschalk + Ash International
AD · Gottschalk + Ash International
D · Fritz Gottschalk, Karin Leibundgut
コンサルタント会社

Cheshire Cat
Bookstore
USA 1985
LaPine/O'Very
AD, D, A · Julia LaPine, Traci O'Very
  Covery
C · Bruce J. Roberts
書店

Kenner Printing Co. Inc.
418 West 25 Street
New York NY 10001
212 8078800

Karen Wong

6525 Sunset Blvd.
Suite 303
Los Angeles
CA 90028

(213) 460-4916

Shimokochi/
Reeves
Design

Mamoru
Shimokochi

STREET
SHOES
↑

841 Lexington Avenue New York City 10021 Telephone 570-0440

Kenner Printing Co., Inc.
USA
C · Karen Wong
印刷会社

Shimokochi/Reeves Design
Graphic design firm
USA 1985
Shimokochi/Reeves Design
AD · Mamoru Shimokochi, Anne Reeves
D · Mamoru Shimokochi
グラフィックデザイン会社

Street Shoes Inc.
Shoe store
USA 1981
Pentagram Design Ltd.
AD · Colin Forbes
D · Dan Friedman
靴店

InterIsland Resorts
USA 1972
Clarence Lee Design
AD, D · Ryo Urano
リゾート

Light Language
Photographic illustration
USA
C · Light Language
イラストレーション

Aoyama Mihoncho
Paper shop
Japan 1989
Shin Matsunaga Design Inc.
AD, D · Shin Matsunaga
C · Takeo Co., Ltd.
紙販売店

Noreen Morioka Design
Designers
USA 1988
Noreen Morioka Design
AD, D · Noreen Morioka
デザインスタジオ

Cabin Fever
Gift and card store
USA 1986
LaPine/O'Very
AD, D, A · Julia LaPine
ギフト商品・カード販売店

James Widdowson Photography
Photographer
Australia 1988
Condon Payne Terry Pty. Ltd.
AD · CPT
D · Clyde Terry
A · Stu-art Wilson
写真家

Holt communications
Public relations and
communication company
USA 1985
Tandem Studios
AD, D, A · Daniel Ruesch
PR 会社

Phantom Records, Inc.
Record company
USA 1974
Milton Glaser, Inc.
AD, D, A · Milton Glaser
レコード会社

Pepper
Fashion boutique
Brazil 1983/84
Ao Lapis Studio (Animus Propaganda)
AD · Rique Nitzsche
D, A · Rique Nitzsche & Duiú
ファッション・ブティック

Postmark
Furniture store
USA 1988
Kathleen Anderson
AD, D · Kathleen Anderson
家具店

212/966 0511

Pamela
Virgilio

67 Vestry Street
New York
NY
1 0 0 1 3
USA

AUNTIE
YUAN

DAVID KEH

AUNTIE YUAN RESTAURANT
1191A FIRST AVENUE
NEW YORK CITY 10021
212·744·4040

Pamela Virgilio
Graphic designer
USA 1982
Pamela Virgilio
AD, D · Pamela Virgilio
グラフィックデザイナー

Auntie Yuan Restaurant
USA
C · Auntie Yuan Restaurant
レストラン

Japonesque, Inc.
Art Gallery
USA 1983
Japonesque, Inc.
AD, D · Koichi Hara
D · Gaku Ohta
アート・ギャラリー

Japonesque

Japonesque, Inc.
Crocker Center·Galleria,
50 Post Street, San Francisco, CA. 94104
Tel. [415] 398-8577

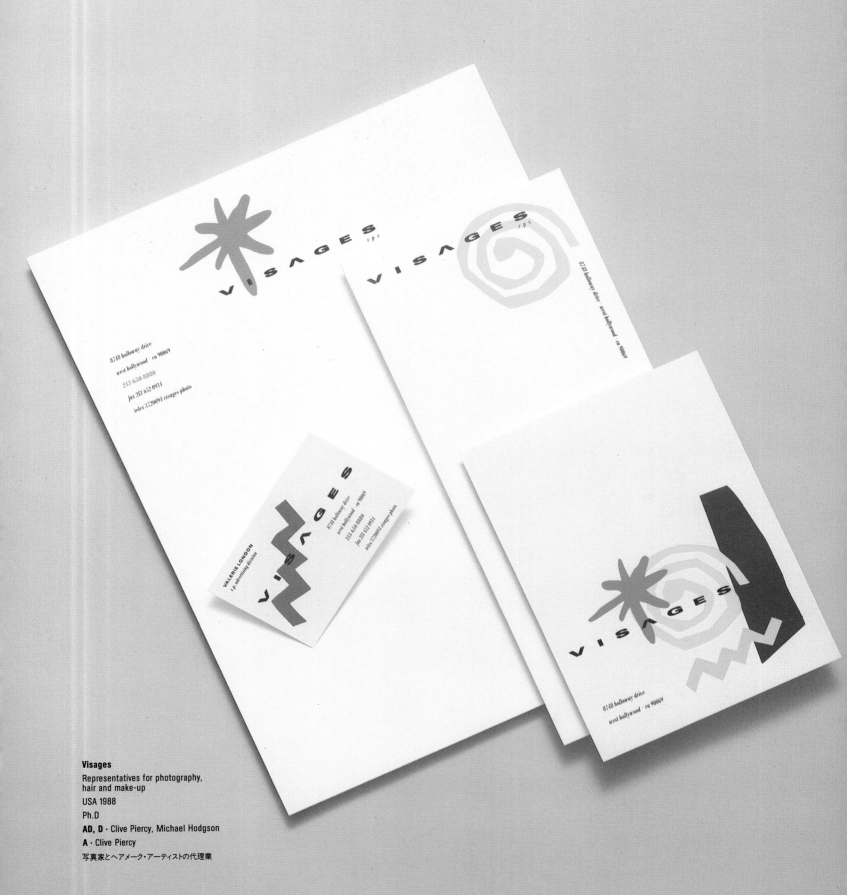

Visages
Representatives for photography,
hair and make-up
USA 1988
Ph.D
AD, D · Clive Piercy, Michael Hodgson
A · Clive Piercy
写真家とヘアメーク・アーティストの代理業

Igarashi International Inc.
Design consultants
USA 1985
Igarashi Studio
AD · Takenobu Igarashi
D · Debi Shimamoto
デザイン・コンサルタント会社

Takenobu Igarashi
International
828 Washington Ave
Santa Monica
California 90403
Tel 213 451 8810
Fax 213 395 9859

Fumiko Igarashi

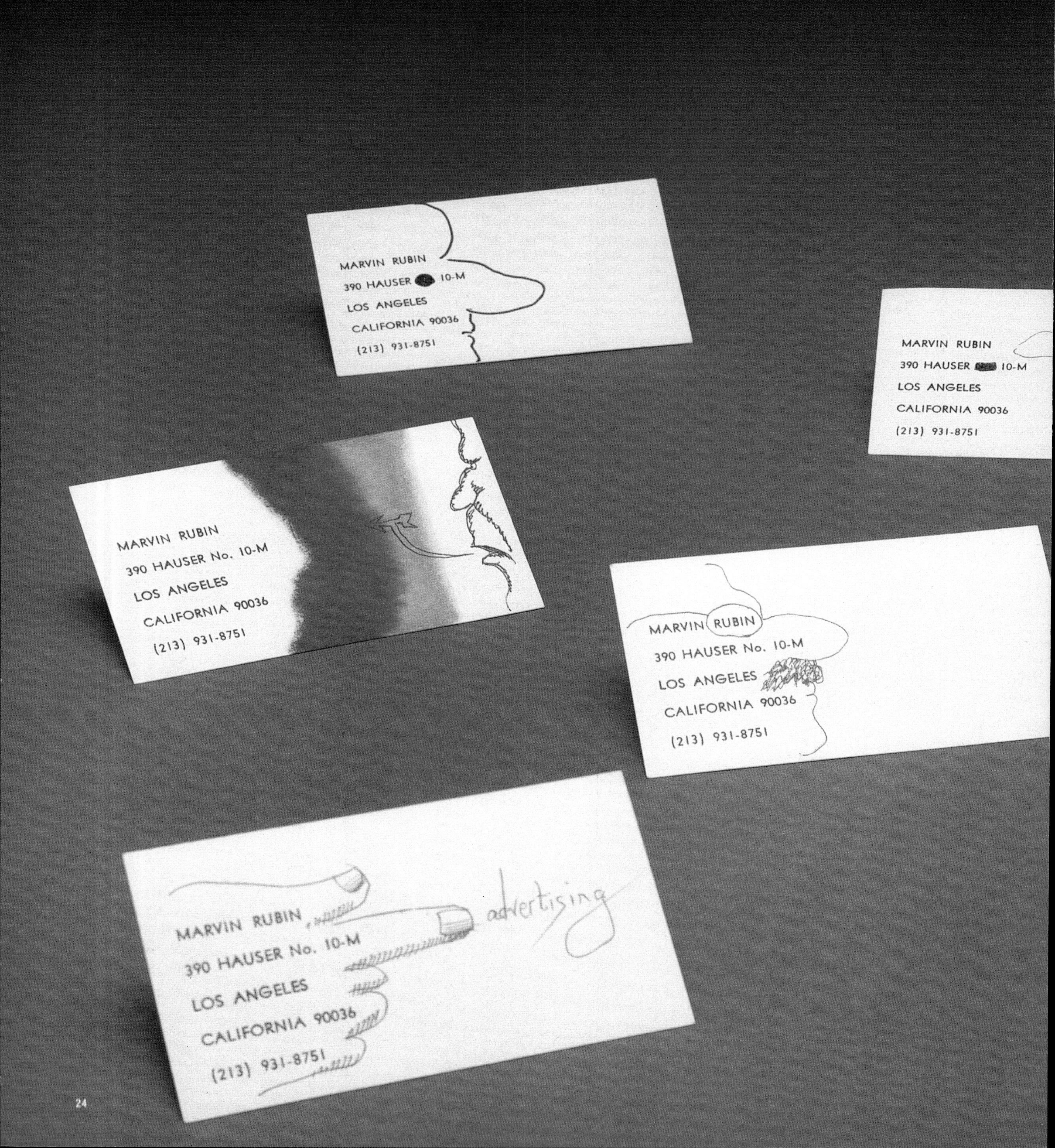

MARVIN RUBIN
390 HAUSER 10-M
LOS ANGELES
CALIFORNIA 90036
(213) 931-8751

MARVIN RUBIN
390 HAUSER 10-M
LOS ANGELES
CALIFORNIA 90036
(213) 931-8751

MARVIN RUBIN
390 HAUSER No. 10-M
LOS ANGELES
CALIFORNIA 90036
(213) 931-8751

MARVIN RUBIN
390 HAUSER No. 10-M
LOS ANGELES
CALIFORNIA 90036
(213) 931-8751

MARVIN RUBIN,
390 HAUSER No. 10-M
LOS ANGELES
CALIFORNIA 90036
(213) 931-8751

advertising

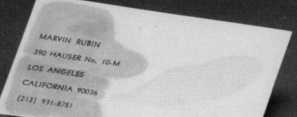

Marvin Rubin
Illustrator
USA
Marvin Rubin
AD, D, A · Marvin Rubin
イラストレーター

v i s i o

v i s i o

v i s i o

H.L. van der Wende
Hoofd Instelling

William Boothlaan 18
3012 VJ Rotterdam
Telefoon (010) 411 16 03

**Regionale Instelling
Zuid-West Nederland**

v i s i o

Visio
Landelijke Stichting
Slechtzienden en Blinden

Landelijke Stichting
Onderwijs
Slechtzienden en Blinden

◎ **Mw. L.R.E.A Wind**
Public Relations en
Voorlichting

Amersfoortsestraatweg 180
1272 RR Huizen
Telefoon (02159) 3 68 08

Visio
Institute for the partially
sighted and blind
Netherlands 1988
Total Design bv
AD, D · Robert van Rixtel
眼の不自由な人のための援助機関

Don Brady
Interior design studio
USA 1983
LaPine/O'Very
AD, D, A · Julia LaPine
インテリアデザイン・スタジオ

DON BRADY
INTERIOR DESIGN
FOUR-THIRTY EAST
SOUTH TEMPLE
SALT LAKE CITY
UTAH, 84111
801-328-0151

KATHY GLASS

DON BRADY
INTERIOR DESIGN
FOUR-THIRTY EAST
SOUTH TEMPLE
SALT LAKE CITY
UTAH, 84111
801-328-0151

KATHY GLASS

DON BRADY
INTERIOR DESIGN
FOUR-THIRTY EAST
SOUTH TEMPLE
SALT LAKE CITY
UTAH, 84111
801-328-0151

KATHY GLASS

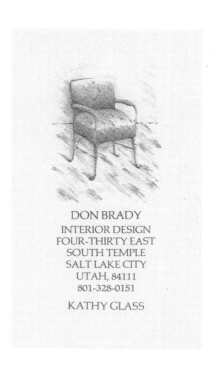

DON BRADY
INTERIOR DESIGN
FOUR-THIRTY EAST
SOUTH TEMPLE
SALT LAKE CITY
UTAH, 84111
801-328-0151

KATHY GLASS

Rod Dyer Group Inc.
Graphic design firm
USA 1988
Rod Dyer Group Inc.
AD · Rod Dyer
D · Steve Twigger
A · Paul Lieth
グラフィックデザイン会社

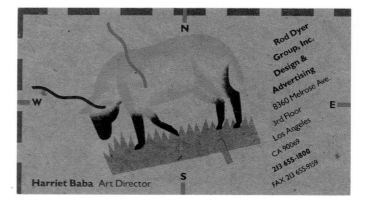

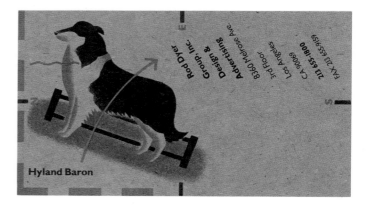

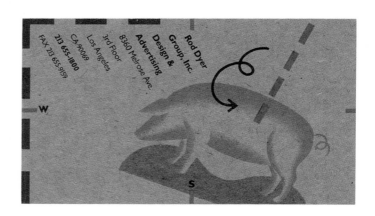

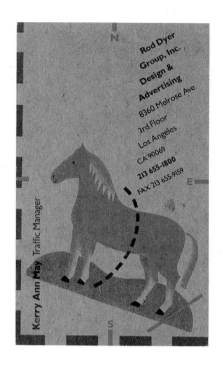

Ao Lapis Studio
Design firm
Brazil 1978
Ao Lapis Studio (Animus Propaganda)
AD, D, A · Rique Nitzsche
デザイン会社

Designwerke
Graphic and product design consultancy
Canada 1983
Smith Boake Designwerke
AD, D · Stephen Boake
A · N.A.
グラフィック／プロダクト・デザイン・コンサルタント

Medina Design
Graphic design firm
Canada 1983
Medina Design
AD, D · Fernando Medina
グラフィックデザイン会社

Monument Properties, Inc.
Real estate broker
USA 1988
Skolos Wedell + Raynor, Inc.
AD, D · Cheryl Lilley
不動産仲介業

Collide Pty. Ltd.
Graphic design firm
Australia 1985
Collide Pty. Ltd.
AD · Clyde Terry
D · Collide
A · Collide/Repromaster
グラフィックデザイン会社

I. D. Corporation
Interior concept company
Japan 1988
Douglas Design Office
AD, D · Douglas Doolittle
インテリア企画会社

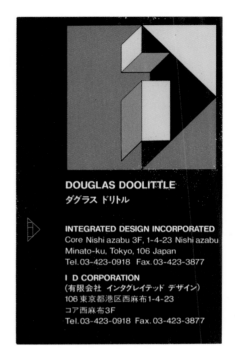

All Australian Graffiti
Illustration and design studio
Australia 1976
All Australian Graffiti
AD, D · Mimmo Cozzolino
A · Megan Williams
イラストレーション/デザイン・スタジオ

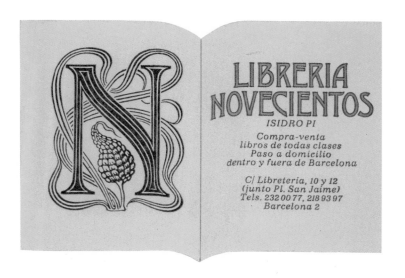

Libreria Novecientos
Old books store
Spain 1978
Enric Huguet
AD, D, A · Enric Huguet
C · Isidro Pi
古書店

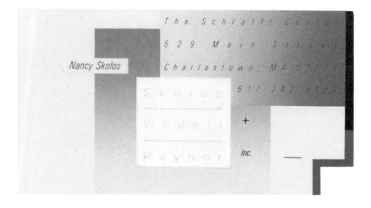

Skolos Wedell + Raynor, Inc.
Graphic design firm
USA 1985
Skolos Wedell + Raynor, Inc.
AD, D · Nancy Skolos
グラフィックデザイン会社

Cucina! Cucina!
Restaurant
USA 1988
Tim Girvin Design
AD, A · Tim Girvin
D · Laurie Vette
C · Schwartz Brothers Restaurants
レストラン

Stichting Ka Geki
Pharmacy
Netherlands 1985
Frans Lieshout
AD, D · Frans Lieshout
薬局

Topey Schwarzenbach
Residential and commercial design
USA 1987
Luci Goodman Studio
AD, D · Luci Goodman
住居/コマーシャル・デザイン

Shooting Gallery East
Graphic arts camera service
USA 1986
Rick Eiber Design
AD · Rick Eiber
D · Rick Eiber, James Mason
写真スタジオ

Sallyanne O'Hanlon & Associates
Interior design firm
Australia 1986
Cato Design Inc. Pty. Ltd.
AD, D · Ken Cato
A · John Papailion
インテリアデザイン会社

Cambridge Furniture Collections
Retail dealer in furniture
USA 1987
Skolos Wedell + Raynor, Inc.
AD, D · Cheryl Lilley
C · Cambridge Furniture Company
家具店

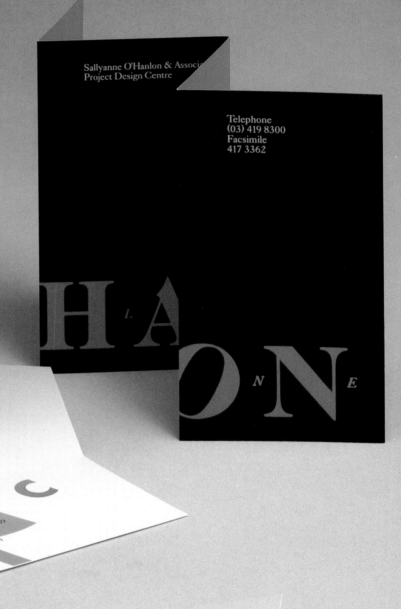

CEFP
Teacher's training center
France 1987
Catherine Zask
AD, D, A · Catherine Zask
教師訓練センター

Theater Without Address
Theater
France 1980
Grapus
AD, D, A · Grapus
C · Pierre Ascaride Théâtre
劇場

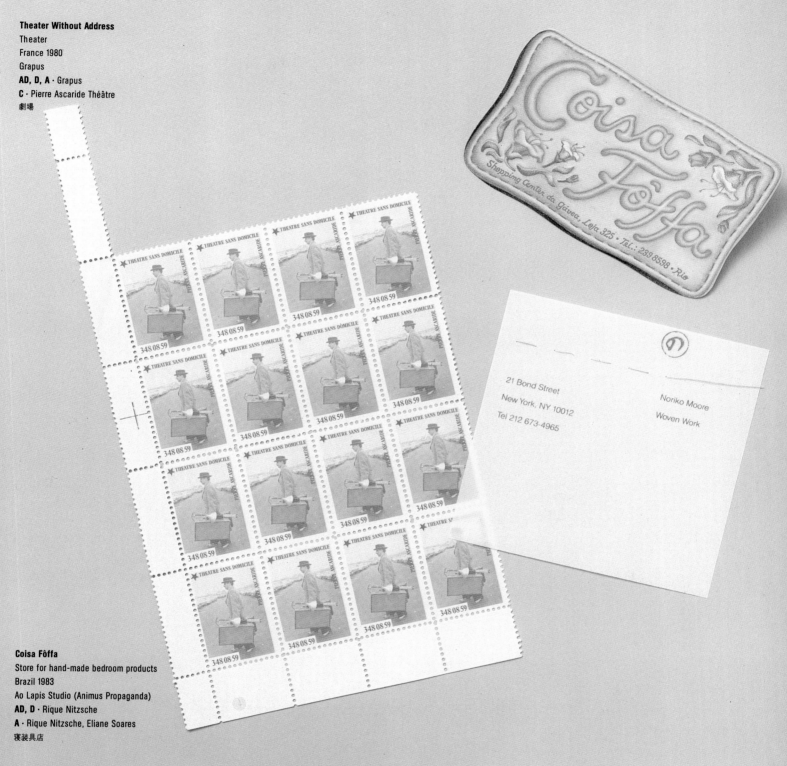

Coisa Fôffa
Store for hand-made bedroom products
Brazil 1983
Ao Lapis Studio (Animus Propaganda)
AD, D · Rique Nitzsche
A · Rique Nitzsche, Eliane Soares
寝装具店

Noriko Moore
Woven goods
USA 1983
Muir Cornelius Moore, Inc.
AD, D · Richard Moore, Noriko Moore
テキスタイルデザイン

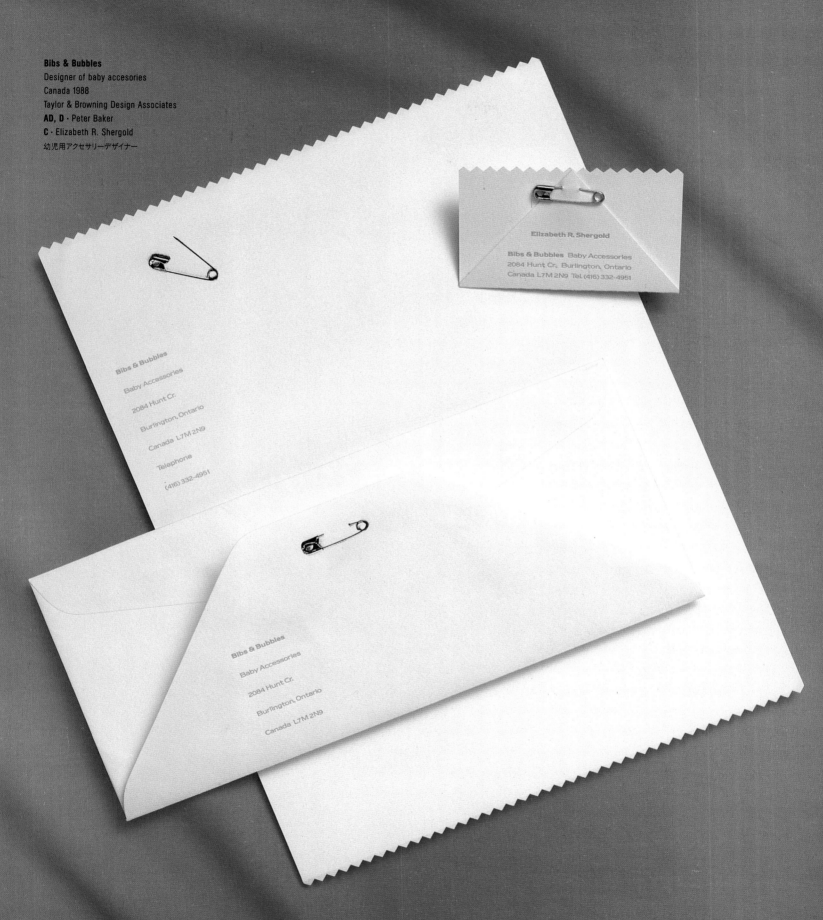

Bibs & Bubbles
Designer of baby accesories
Canada 1988
Taylor & Browning Design Associates
AD, D · Peter Baker
C · Elizabeth R. Shergold
幼児用アクセサリーデザイナー

Elizabeth R. Shergold

Bibs & Bubbles Baby Accessories
2084 Hunt Cr., Burlington, Ontario
Canada L7M 2N9 Tel. (416) 332-4951

Bibs & Bubbles

Baby Accessories

2084 Hunt Cr.

Burlington, Ontario

Canada L7M 2N9

Telephone

(416) 332-4951

Bibs & Bubbles

Baby Accessories

2084 Hunt Cr.

Burlington, Ontario

Canada L7M 2N9

Bruce Wayne
Personal management
USA
C · Bruce Wayne
個人管理コンサルタント

Composition Arts Company
Typography
USA
C · Composition Arts Company
タイポグラフィ

Bruce Wayne
Personal Management

9381 W. Olympic Boulevard
Beverly Hills, California 90212

(213) 553-7570

Mario
Casarini

Composition
Arts
Company

1015 N. Fairfax, Los Angeles,
California 90046 · (213) 654-6034

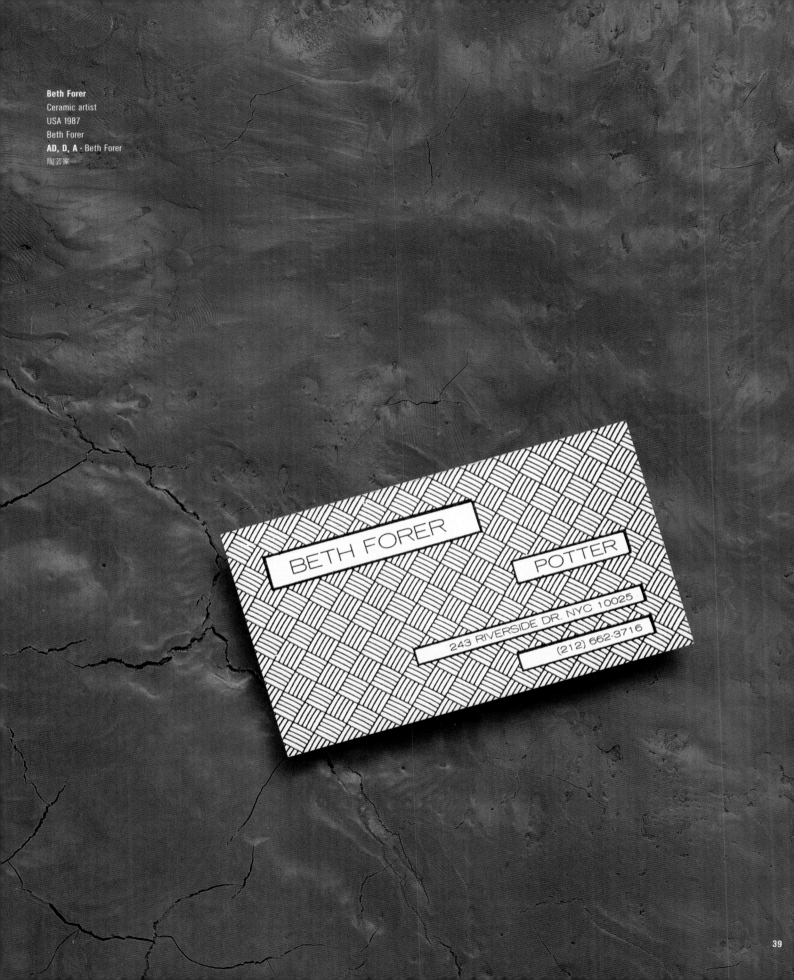

Beth Forer
Ceramic artist
USA 1987
Beth Forer
AD, D, A · Beth Forer
陶芸家

BETH FORER

POTTER

243 RIVERSIDE DR. NYC 10025

(212) 662-3716

Square One Preschool

Kathryn Wauters
Director

413 North 7th Avenue

Phoenix, Arizona 85007

602-252-0230

Square One Preschool

Kathryn Wauters
Director

413 North 7th Avenue

Phoenix, Arizona 85007

602-252-0230

Square One Preschool

Kathryn Wauters
Director

413 North 7th Avenue

Phoenix, Arizona 85007

602-252-0230

Roberts Jones Associates, Inc.
Architects
USA
C · Roberts Jones Associates, Inc.
建築設計事務所

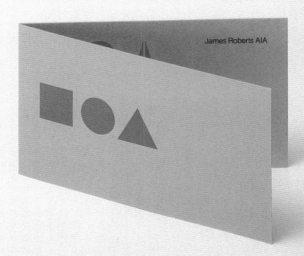

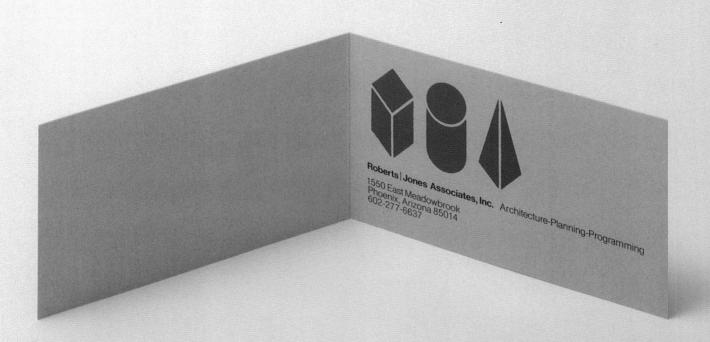

Embrey Press
Printing & Lithography company
USA 1986
Glen Iwasaki
AD, D · Glen Iwasaki
印刷会社

Giuliano
USA
C · Giuliano
業種不明

42

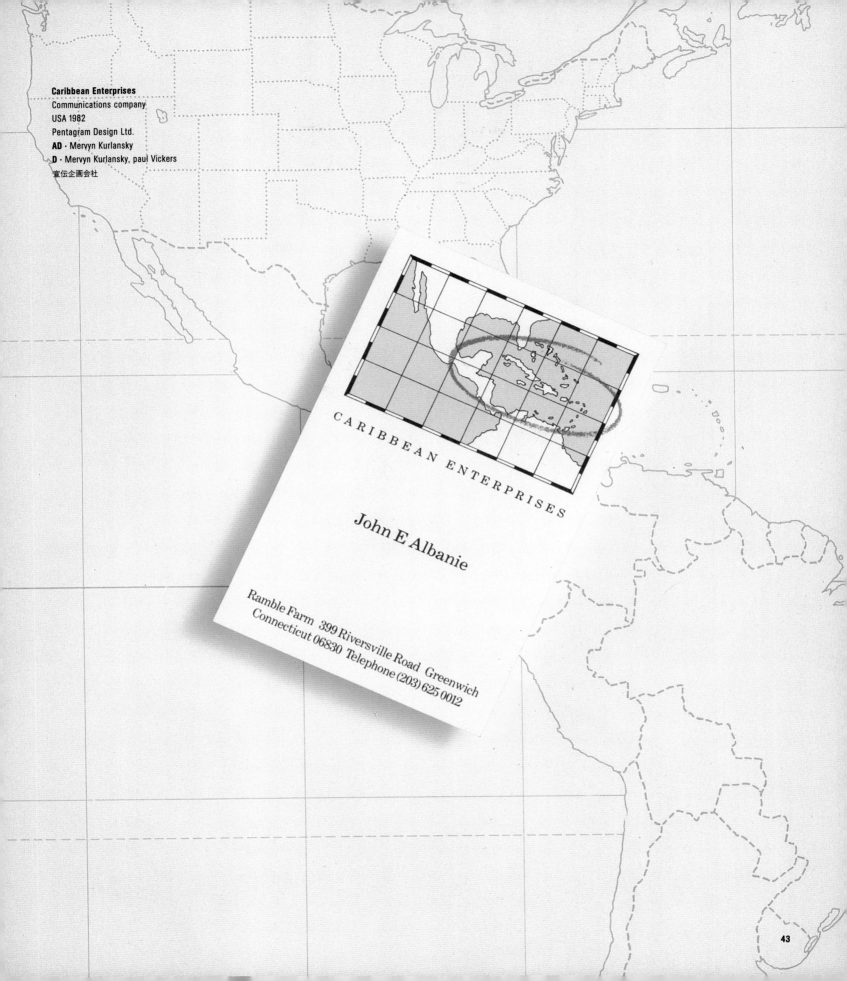

Caribbean Enterprises
Communications company
USA 1982
Pentagram Design Ltd.
AD · Mervyn Kurlansky
D · Mervyn Kurlansky, paul Vickers
宣伝企画会社

CARIBBEAN ENTERPRISES

John E Albanie

Ramble Farm 399 Riversville Road Greenwich
Connecticut 06830 Telephone (203) 625 0012

KEATON DESIGN

JAMES KEATON

541 ELEVENTH STREET, SOUTHEAST
WASHINGTON, DC 20003 202 547 4422

SEGD

John Muhlhausen, President

Society of Environmental
Graphic Designers
1146 Green Street
Roswell, GA 30075
404 642-1146

acti

Robert T. Wormald

Vice President

Eight Farm Springs
Farmington, CT 06032

(203) 674-8817

a DNA company

Keaton Design
Graphic designer
USA 1983
GK+D Communications Inc.
AD, D · James Keaton
A · Hilary Gardner
グラフィックデザイナー

SEGD
USA 1987
D · Matthew Bartholomew
C · Society of Environmental Graphic
Designers
環境グラフィックデザイン団体

acti
USA
C · acti
業種不明

Junn Paasche-Aasen Design
Design firm
Norway 1983
Junn Paasche-Aasen Design
AD, D · Junn Paasche-Aasen
デザイン会社

Prime Design
Graphic designer
Australia 1987
Prime Design
AD, D · Dennis Veal
A · Monica Krueger
グラフィックデザイナー

Debi Shimamoto
Graphic designer
Japan 1985
AD, D · Debi Shimamoto
グラフィックデザイナー

JOSEPH
pour la maison

16 Sloane Street, London SW1. 01-235 9868

Judi Schoenback
Stylist
USA 1972
Federico Design
AD, D · Gene Federico
スタイリスト

Bishop Color Inc.
Photo retoucher
USA 1972
Federico Design
AD, D, A · Gene Federico
写真レタッチ会社

William Zemanek
Photographer
USA 1988
Gillian/Craig Associates
AD, D · Craig Sheumaker
写真家

WILLIAM ZEMANEK PHOTOGRAPHY
415 861 5557

WILLIAM ZEMANEK
PHOTOGRAPHY
415 861 5557

165 8TH STREET #310
SAN FRANCISCO CA 94103

WILLIAM ZEMANEK PHOTOGRAPHY
165 8TH STREET #310
SAN FRANCISCO CA 94103

MELINDA MARCUS

MARCUS & ASSOCIATES INC.

6022 Meadow Crest Drive

Dallas, Texas 75230

214 987 3060

LORI BARNETT DESIGN.
300 BRANNAN SUITE 311
SAN FRANCISCO, CA. 94107
4 1 5 . 5 4 3 . 2 3 3 0

Marcus & Associates Inc.
Advertising agency
USA 1985
Richards Brock Miller Mitchell &
Associates
D - Danny Kamerath
広告代理店

Lori Barnett Design
Graphic design firm
USA 1988
Lori Barnett Design
AD, D - Lori Barnett
グラフィックデザイン会社

MICHAEL MABRY DESIGN

212 SUTTER
SAN FRANCISCO
CA 94108
415 982 7336

MICHAEL MABRY

ILLUSTRATION

H E R S E Y
J O R S E N Y
1930 Hyde St., No. 1 SF CA 94109
415-928-6553

Florence
Wong
Artist
835 Elmira Drive
Sunnyvale
California
94087
408 739 8951

Michael Mabry Design
Design firm
USA 1984
Michael Mabry Design
AD, D · Michael Mabry
A · Peter Soe
デザイン会社

John Hersey
Illustrator
USA
A · John Hersey
C · John Hersey
イラストレーター

Florence Wong
Artist
USA 1988
Glen Randle
AD, D · Glen Randle
アーティスト

ORIS YAMASHITA
GRAPHIC DESIGN
707 ROBINSON STREET
LOS ANGELES, CALIFORNIA 90026
213.666.8263

Gregory Thomas
& Associates

1552 18th Street
Santa Monica, California
90404
213.828.5884

The Davis Group

Design Division

Sancho

Vice President

160 Roy Street, Seattle, WA 98109

Telephone 206·282-2422

Oris Yamashita
Graphic designer
USA 1984
C · Oris Yamashita
グラフィックデザイナー

Gregory Thomas & Associates
Design consultants
USA
Gregory Thomas & Associates
AD, D · Gregory Thomas
デザインコンサルタント会社

The Davis Group
Graphic design firm
USA 1986
The Davis Group
AD, D · Sancho
グラフィックデザイン会社

Henry Anton Knudsen
Graphic designer
Denmark
C - Henry Anton Knudsen
グラフィックデザイナー

HENRY ANTON KNUDSEN
GRAPHIC DESIGNER I.D.D.

BALDERSGADE 77
2200 COPENHAGEN
DENMARK

Restaurant Katsu
Japanese restaurant
USA 1981
AD · Mineo Mizuno
D · Katsu Michite
日本食レストラン

Jim Heimann Design
Design firm
USA
C · Jim Heimann Design
デザイン会社

japanese cuisine
restaurant KATSU
1972 hillhurst
los angeles
calif 90027
213 665 1891

MASON & SCOTT

Les Mason

Graphic Design
& Advertising

Suite 11
Queens Building
97 William Street
Perth. 6000
Western Australia

Telephone
(09) 481 0700

THANE ROBERTS
ARCHITECTURAL DESIGN
SOLAR CONSULTATION
602B ASHLAND AVE
SANTA MONICA
CALIFORNIA 90405
396-6858 396-2002

Mason & Scott
Graphic design firm
Australia
C · Mason & Scott
グラフィックデザイン会社

Thane Roberts
Architectural designer
USA 1982
Thane Roberts, AIA
AD, D, A · Thane Roberts
建築デザイナー

Mike Fink
Commercial artist
USA 1980
Mike Fink
AD, D, A · Mike Fink
グラフィックデザイナー

Travel Trunk
Travel agency
England 1985
Pentagram Design Ltd.
AD · John McConnell
D · John McConnell, John Rushworth
A · John Rushworth
旅行代理店

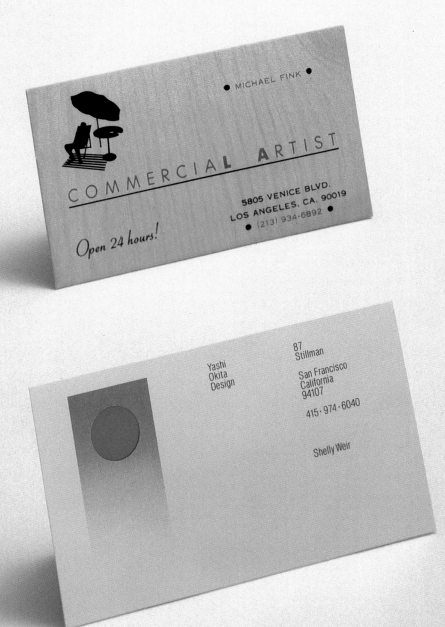

Yashi Okita Design
Design firm
USA
Yashi Okita Design
AD, D · Yashi Okita Design
デザイン会社

Next, Inc.
Computer manufacturer
USA 1985
Paul Rand, Inc.
AD, D, A · Paul Rand
コンピュータ会社

Tokiwa Printing Co., Ltd.
Japan 1983
Igarashi Studio
AD · Takenobu Igarashi
D · Hiromi Nakata
印刷会社

Creative Catering, Inc.
USA
C · Creative Catering, Inc.
ケイタリング会社

Todo Mundo
Film and music production company
USA 1988
M & Co.
AD · Tibor Kalman
D · Emily Oberman
A · Maira Kalman
映画/音楽プロダクション

TODO MUNDO, LTD. BOX 47 PRINCE STREET STATION NEW YORK, NY 10012 (212) 334-5110 (FAX) 219-8664

TODO MUNDO, LTD. BOX 47 PRINCE STREET STATION NEW YORK 10012

(212) 334-5110
(FAX) 219-8664

NEW YORK, NY
10012

TODO MUNDO, LTD.
BOX 47 PRINCE STREET STATION

WORDS   PICTURES

Corzo & von Kalinowski

Alvaro A. Corzo

1245 Roslyn Lane
La Jolla, California 92037
619·454·9939

Corzo & von Kalinowski
Industrial design firm
USA 1982
Wayne Hunt Design, Inc.
AD · Wayne Hunt
D · Norma O'Neill
インダストリアルデザイン会社

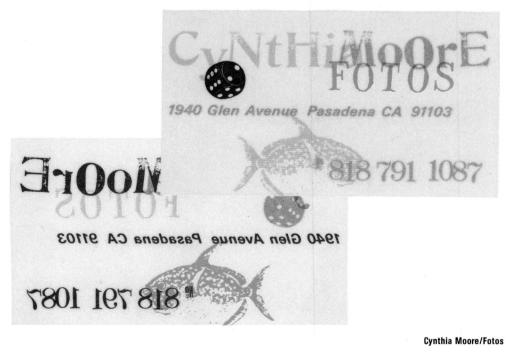

Cynthia Moore/Fotos
Photographer
USA 1985
Luci Goodman Studio
AD, D · Luci Goodman
写真家

The Silk Purse Company

Christopher Higgins ARICS
The Silk Purse Company Ltd
5 The Square Winchester SO23 9ES
Tel: Winchester (0962) 63603

IMAGE WORKSHOP
THE ART OF COMPUTER DESIGN FOR PRINT

Enzo Finger & Petter Winsnes
Design and photography
Norway 1986
Enzo Finger & petter Winsnes
AD, D · Enzo Finger
デザイン/写真事務所

The Silk Purse Co., Ltd.
Architectural computer software
company
England 1986
The Partners (Design Consultants) Ltd.
AD · Malcolm Swatridge
D · Martin Devlin
建築コンピュータソフト会社

The Image Workshop Ltd.
Computer graphics company
England 1987
Lloyd Northover Ltd.
AD · Jim Northover
D · Malcolm Farrar
コンピュータグラフィックス会社

Rique Nitzsche
Graphic designer
Brazil 1976
AD, D, A · Rique Nitzsche
グラフィックデザイナー

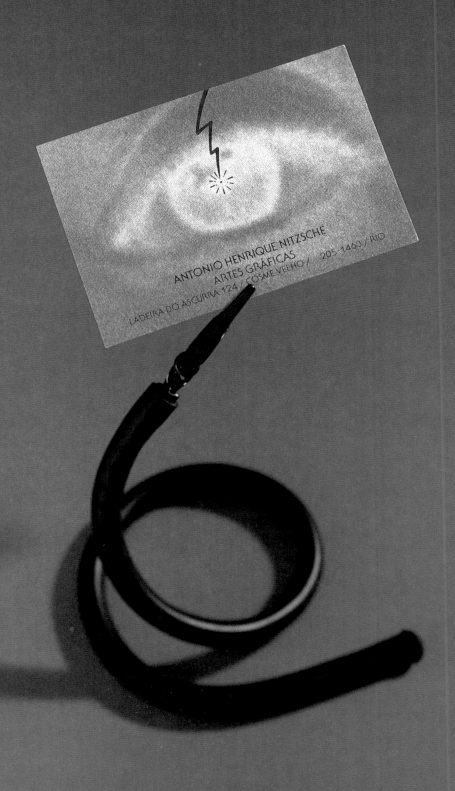

Kargah Aks
Iran 1985
Momayez Studio
AD, D, A · Morteza Momayez
業種不明

Coley Poter Bell
Design consultancy
England 1987
Coley Poter Bell
AD · Colin Poter
D · Kate Shaw
デザイン・コンサルタント

Vase Limited
Florists
England 1988
Design House Consultants Ltd.
AD · Chris Lower
D · Rosanna Bianchini
A · Andy Seymour
花屋

Michael Barrie
Mens wear retail chain
England 1985
Michael Peters Group PLC
AD, D · Madeleine Bennett
紳士服店

Frills
Custom window treatment service
USA 1986
Zender + Associates, Inc.
AD, D, A · David Steinbrunner
C · Margaret Wilson Campbell
オーダー・カーテン会社

Elite Jewels
USA 1986
Luci Goodman Studio
AD, D · Luci Goodman
宝石商

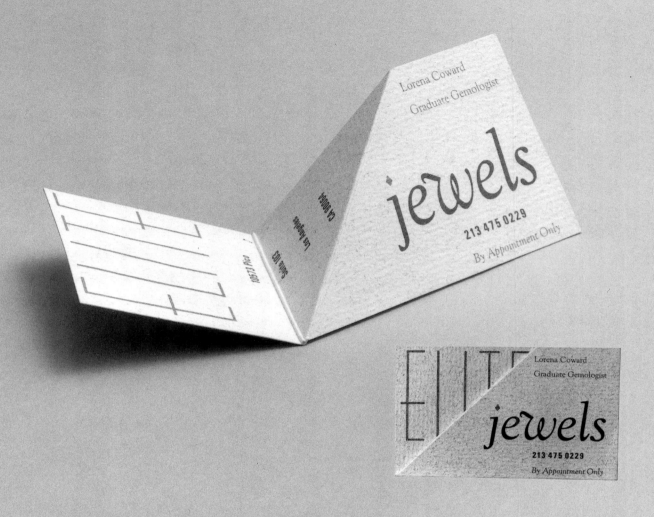

Da Alfredo Ristorante
Restaurant
West Germany 1986
Lang Art + Graphic-Deisgn
AD, D, A · Hans-Georg Lang
レストラン

Loebl Schlossman and Hackl
John I. Schlossman FAIA
Principal
ARCHITECTS
845 North Michigan Avenue
Chicago, Illinois 60611
Telephone 312 337 5800

16 0 16 32 48 64 80 96 112 128 144

Tim hartford
Graphic design
6030 north sheridan
Apartment 1104
Chicago illinois 60660
Phone 312 784 3851

Metropolitan Park
1100 Olive Way, Suite 1560
Seattle, Washington 98101
Phone 206.682.8235
Fax 206.623.0528

MAGICMATION

Cynthia M. Chin
Production Manager

Loebl Schlossman and Hackl
Architects
USA 1987
Rick Eiber Design
AD, D · Rick Eiber
建築設計事務所

Tim Hartford Graphic Design
USA 1988
Timothy Hartford
AD, D · Timothy Hartford
グラフィックデザイン会社

Magicmation
Computer graphics firm
USA 1988
M Design
AD, D · Glenn Mitsui, Jesse Doquilo
A · Glenn Mitsui
コンピュータグラフィックス会社

Celia Keyworth
Freelance cook
England 1987
Pentagram Design Ltd.
AD, D · John Rushworth
A · N/A
料理研究家

Bezalel
Academy of arts and design Jerusalem
Israel
エルサレム・芸術・デザイン・アカデミー

Rodeo Collection
Retail shopping center
USA 1978
Bass/Yager and Associates
AD, D · Saul Bass
A · Saul Bass, Art Goodman
ショッピングセンター

Celia Keyworth
11 Charlton Kings Road
London, NW5 2SB
Telephone 01 267 8872

bezalel
academy of arts & design jerusalem
1 bezalel street jerusalem 94591
telephones 02·223121·2·3
graphic design department
telephone 02·223124 telex 26452
prof. yarom vardimon
telephones 02·722092 03·239361

RODEO COLLECTION

Massimo Vignelli
Executive Consultant

OUN International Limited
Seventh Minami Aoyama Bldg.
7-12-14 Minami Aoyama
Minato-ku, Tokyo 107 Japan
Tel 03-486-1011/Fax 03-486-1900
Telex J27495 OUNTKY

Lettergraphics SA Pty Ltd
Design Consultants
and Manufacturers
of Architectural Graphics
and Signage

OUN International Ltd.
Design agency
Japan 1987
Igarashi Studio
AD · Takenobu Igarashi
D · Debi Shimamoto
デザイン・エージェンシー

Lettergraphics SA Pty. Ltd.
Design consultants
Australia 1985
Barrie Tucker Design
AD · Barrie Tucker
デザイン・コンサルタント会社

CASADO

John Casado

Casado Design 50 Green Street San Francisco Ca 94111 Phone 415.397.5345

200 East Culver Boulevard
Playa Del Rey, California 90291
(213) 823-0975

Robert Miles Runyan
Chairman of the Board

Runyan+Rice

Casado Design
Design firm
USA
Casado Design
AD, D · John Casado
デザイン会社

Robert Miles Runyan & Associates
Design firm
USA 1982
Robert Miles Runyan & Associates
AD, D, A · Robert Miles Runyan
デザイン会社

MIRANDA SPITTELER

IN AID OF INTERMEDIATE TECHNOLOGY

WEST INDIA HOUSE · MILLWALL DOCK · LONDON E14 9TJ · TELEPHONE 01–515 3000 ·

The Road Butler, Inc.

Cynthia Van de Walker
President

6900 Airport Rd.
P.O. Box 66
Malton, Ontario L4V 1E8

Telephone
Dispatch   677-0087
Administration 962-4078

WILL GILLIS / *wordsmith*
1440 North Gardner / #206
Los Angeles, California / 90046
(213) 876-0452

Four Corners World Bike Ride
Charity organization
England 1988
Michael Peters Group PLC
AD · Glenn Tutssel
D, A · Mark Lloyd
慈善団体

The Road Butler, Inc.
Canada
C · The Road Butler, Inc.
業種不明

Will Gillis
USA
C · Will Gillis
業種不明

مرتضی ممیز: طراح گرافیک
Morteza MOMAYEZ
Graphic Designer

شماره ۳۷ کوچه ششم
خیابان پاکستان
عباس‌آباد تهران ۱۵
37.6th alley
Pakistan Str.
Tehran 15 IRAN

مرتضی ممیز
شماره ۳۷ کوچه ششم
خیابان پاکستان
عباس‌آباد تهران ۱۵

Morteza MOMAYEZ
37.6th alley
Pakistan Str.
Tehran 15 IRAN

Morteza Momayez
Graphic designer
Iran 1978
Momayez Studio
AD, D, A · Morteza Momayez
グラフィックデザイナー

Grapus
Graphic design firm
France 1986–88
Grapus
AD, D, A · Grapus
グラフィックデザイン会社

Murray Duitz
Photographer
USA 1968
Federico Design
AD, D · Gene Federico
写真家

Perfumes Floriberia, S.A.
Cosmetics/Perfumery
Spain 1977
Enric Huguet
AD, D, A · Enric Huguet
C · A. Puig, S.A.
化粧品・香水会社

Forma
Photographers' representative
USA 1969
Federico Design
AD, D · Gene Federico
写真家代理業

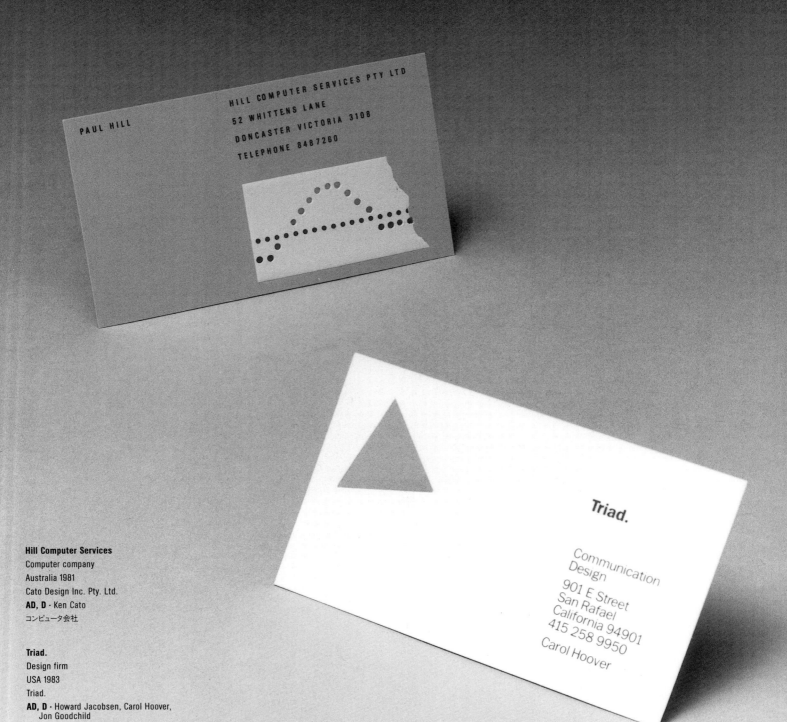

Hill Computer Services
Computer company
Australia 1981
Cato Design Inc. Pty. Ltd.
AD, D · Ken Cato
コンピュータ会社

Triad.
Design firm
USA 1983
Triad.
AD, D · Howard Jacobsen, Carol Hoover,
  Jon Goodchild
デザイン会社

Cary Company
USA
C · Cary Company
業種不明

(213) 379-0264

MITS KATAOKA / 920 8th PLACE, HERMOSA BEACH, CALIF. 90254

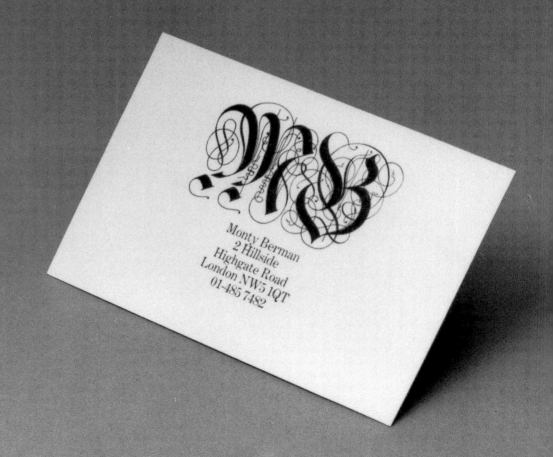

Monty Berman
2 Hillside
Highgate Road
London NW5 1QT
01-485 7482

Mits Kataoka
Personal business card
USA
C · Mits Kataoka
個人用名刺

Monty & Myrtle Berman
Personal business card
England 1981
Pentagram Design Ltd.
AD · Mervyn Kurlansky
D · Mervyn Kurlansky, Paul Vickers
A · Wold Spoerl
個人用名刺

Ernest T. Nagamatsu, D.D.S., Inc.

1245 Wilshire Boulevard, Suite 903
Los Angeles, California 90017
(213) 481-1420

Steven A. Heller

5808

Nagle Ave.

Van Nuys

California

91401

818 901 1067

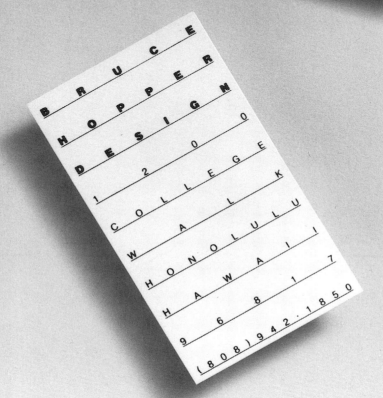

Ernest T. Nagamatsu
Dentist
USA 1987
Ernest T. Nagamatsu, D.D.S., Inc.
AD, D · Ernest T. Nagamatsu
A · Colleen Hendrickson
歯科医師

Steven A. Heller
Photographer
USA 1988
AD, D · Dan McNulty
写真家

Bruce Hopper Design
Graphic/Architectural designer
USA 1984
Bruce Hopper Design
AD, D · Bruce Hopper
グラフィック/建築デザイナー

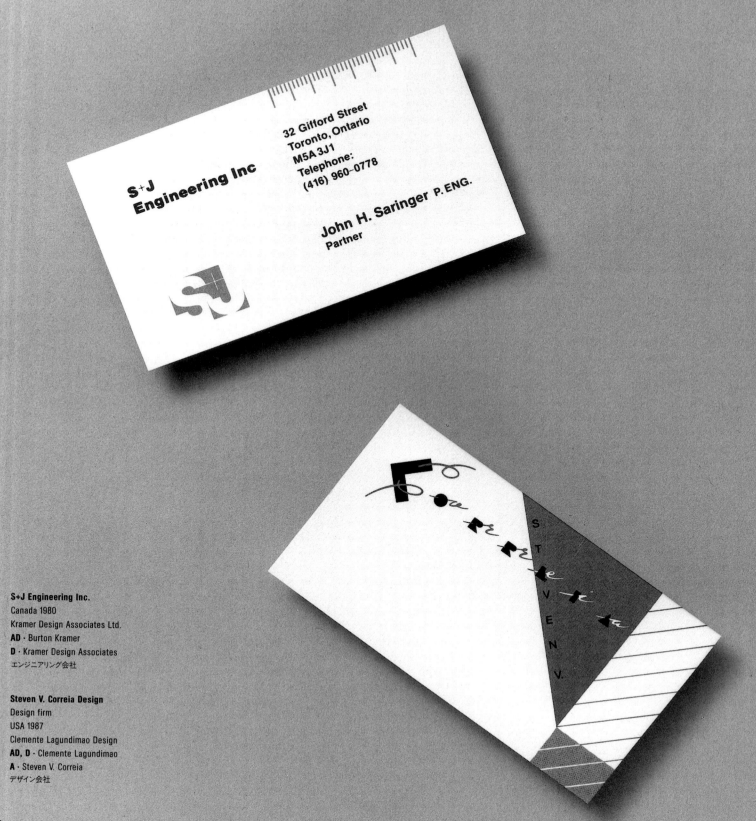

S+J
Engineering Inc

32 Gifford Street
Toronto, Ontario
M5A 3J1
Telephone:
(416) 960-0778

John H. Saringer P. ENG.
Partner

S+J Engineering Inc.
Canada 1980
Kramer Design Associates Ltd.
AD · Burton Kramer
D · Kramer Design Associates
エンジニアリング会社

Steven V. Correia Design
Design firm
USA 1987
Clemente Lagundimao Design
AD, D · Clemente Lagundimao
A · Steven V. Correia
デザイン会社

Railex Rail Line
Fictitious card for a paper company
USA 1985
AD, D · Woody Pirtle
A · N/A
C · Simpson Paper Co.
紙会社のための試作

Yachtours Limited
England 1980
Pentagram Design Ltd.
AD · John McConnell
D · John McConnell, David Stuart,
Keren House
A · Mel Calman
ヨットツアー会社

Pat Taylor Inc.
Graphic design studio
USA 1984
Pat Taylor Inc.
AD, D · Pat Taylor
グラフィックデザイン・スタジオ

railex

Railex Rail Line
1000 North Lindberg
St. Louis, Missouri 63044
(312) 731-2200

Paul Armstrong

Anthony Nielson
YACHTOURS LIMITED
48 Westbourne Park Road
London W2 5BH
Telephone 01 229 9983
Telex 268991

PAT TAYLOR INC 3540 S STREET NW WASHINGTON DC 20007 (202) 338-0962

Hilton International Brisbane
Hotel
Australia 1986
Barrie Tucker Design
AD · Barrie Tucker
D · Mark Janetzki
A · Brenton Hill
ホテル

HILTON
INTERNATIONAL
BRISBANE

HILTON
INTERNATIONAL
BRISBANE

DAVID F HOROVITZ
GENERAL MANAGER

HILTON
INTERNATIONAL
BRISBANE

ELIZABETH
GPO BOX
TELEPHON

Alice Martin
Stylist
USA 1968
Federico Design
AD, D · Gene Federico
スタイリスト

Joe Cahill
Photographers' representative
USA 1970
Federico Design
AD, D · Gene Federico
写真家代理業

M'COM
Minitel
France 1987
Grapus
AD, D, A · Grapus
ミニテル

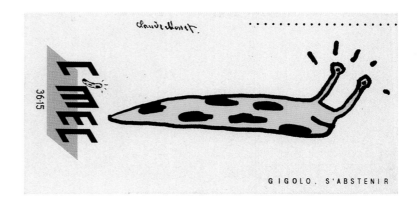

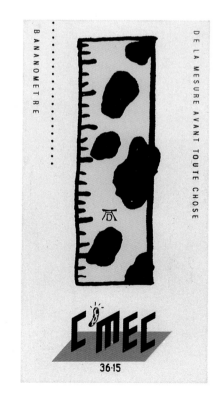

Eddie Lau Co., Ltd.
Fashion boutique
Hong Kong 1986
Alan Chan Design Co.
AD · Alan Chan
D · Alan Chan, Alvin Chan
ファッション・ブティック

Ka Cheong Antique
Hong Kong 1988
Alan Chan Design Co.
AD · Alan Chan
D · Alan Chan, Phillip Leung, Andy Ip
アンティーク店

Polygon Pictures
Film production company
Japan 1987
Igarashi Studio
AD · Takenobu Igarashi
D · Yukimi Sasago
映画プロダクション

Larry Jewelry
Hong Kong 1987
Kan Tai-keung Design & Associates Ltd.
AD · Kan Tai-keung
D · Johnson Wong
宝石商

Max's
Restaurant
Australia 1986
Flett Henderson & Arnold
AD · Richard Henderson
D, A · Flett Henderson & Arnold
C · Hyatt On Collins Hotel
レストラン

Lee Stout
Interior designer
USA 1986
David Curry Design Inc.
AD, D · David Curry
インテリアデザイナー

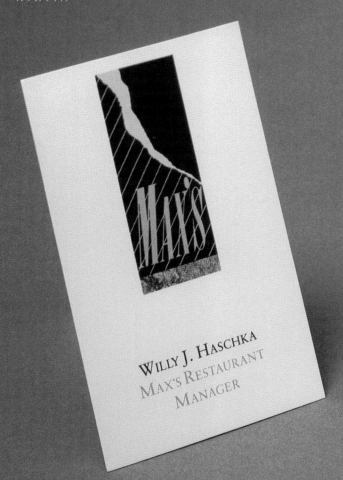

The Rec Club
Health club
Australia 1987
Barrie Tucker Design
AD · Barrie Tucker
D · Mark Janetzki
A · Meltssa Puust
C · Sanctuary Cove Resort
ヘルス・クラブ

Rex
Printing company
Japan 1987
Igarashi Studio
AD · Takenobu Igarashi
D · Honami Morita
印刷会社

Osama Scrittura S.p.A.
Ball-point pen company
Italy 1988
Studio "Visual Due"
AD, D · Vittorio Prina
ボールペン会社

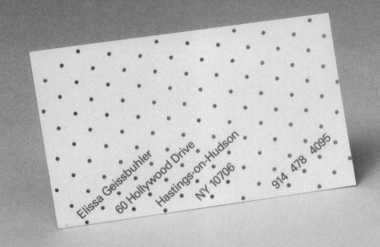

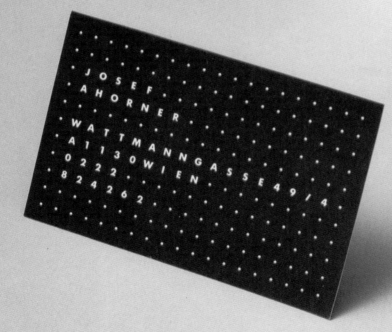

Elissa Geissbuhler
Costume jewelry
USA 1987
Steff Geissbuhler
AD, D, A · Steff Geissbuhler
装身具デザイナー

Iris Moar
Personal business card
Australia 1987
Flett Henderson & Arnold
AD · Richard Henderson
D, A · Flett Henderson & Arnold
個人用名刺

Josef Ahorner
Personal business card
Austria 1985
Harry Metzler Artdesign
AD, D, A · Harry Metzler
個人用名刺

Shimokochi/Reeves Design
Graphic design firm
USA 1989
Shimokochi/Reeves Design
AD · Mamoru Shimokochi
D · Mamoru Shimokochi
A · Mamoru Shimokochi, Kathryn Walker
グラフィックデザイン会社

Yosemite Institute
Educational institute
USA 1985
Akagi Design
AD · Doug Akagai
D · Doug Akagi, Sharrie Brooks
C · Yosemite National Institutes
教育研究所

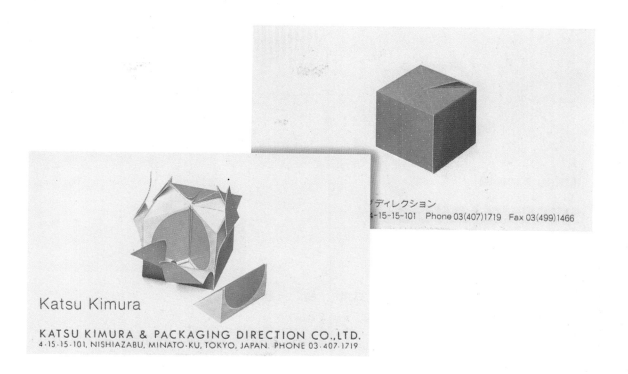

ディレクション
4-15-15-101　Phone 03(407)1719　Fax 03(499)1466

Katsu Kimura

KATSU KIMURA & PACKAGING DIRECTION CO.,LTD.
4·15·15·101, NISHIAZABU, MINATO·KU, TOKYO, JAPAN. PHONE 03·407·1719

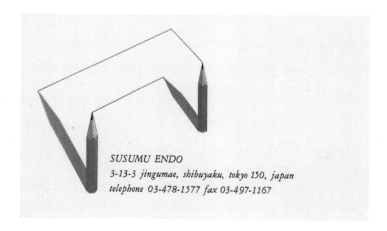

SUSUMU ENDO
3-13-3 jingumae, shibuyaku, tokyo 150, japan
telephone 03-478-1577 fax 03-497-1167

Katsu Kimura
Package designer
Japan 1985
Katsu Kimura & Packaging Direction
AD, D · Katsu Kimura
パッケージデザイナー

Susumu Endo
Graphic designer
Japan 1987
Susumu Endo
AD, D · Susumu Endo
グラフィックデザイナー

Gallimaufry
Design store
USA
C · Gallimaufry
デザイン・ショップ

Mondo Typo, Inc.
Typesetting company
USA 1987
Mondo Typo, Inc.
AD, D · Joe Molloy
写植会社

Zazana Licko Design
Design firm
USA 1987
Zazana Licko Design
AD, D · Zazana Licko
デザイン会社

Gini Graphics, Inc.
Graphic design studio
USA 1987
Gini Graphics, Inc.
AD, D, A · Girish Patel
グラフィックデザイン・スタジオ

Modern Living
Furniture store
USA 1987
O'Mara/Saitz
AD · John Zabrucky
D · Dan O'Mara
A · Robert Commander
家具店

Invetech
Design firm
Australia 1987
Invetech Design
AD · Mary Jane Taylor
D, A · Invetech Design Team
デザイン会社

Canfield Company
Commercial brokerage
USA 1986
Shimokochi/Reeves Design
AD · Mamoru Shimokochi, Anne Reeves
D · Mamoru Shimokochi
コマーシャル・ブローカー

Barnes Neon Signs Pty. Ltd.
Australia 1985
Barnes Publicity
AD, D, A · Lindi Warner
ネオンサイン会社

Holiday Junction Corporation
Travel franchise
Canada 1985
Raymond Lee & Associates Ltd.
AD, D · Raymond Lee
A · Derek Chung Tiam Fook
旅行会社

Future Fund Shares Inc.
Investment fund
Canada 1984
Smith Boake Designwerke
AD, D · Stephen Boake
A · N.A.
投資会社

Woolies
Clothing company
USA 1986
Carron Design
AD · Ross Carron
D · Ross Carron, Joann Maass
衣料品会社

American Corporate Services, Inc.
Computer office systems
USA 1986
The Appelbaum Company
AD, D · Harvey Appelbaum
コンピュータ・オフィス・システム会社

DIE HARRISONS
ARTISTIK UNSERER ZEIT

HARRY BRANDEL JUNIOR
BRESLAUER STRASSE 6
7032 SINDELFINGEN
TELEFON 0 70 31 / 87 02 57 ∅

The Harrisons
Entertainment company
West Germany 1986/87
Lang Art + Graphic-Design
AD, D, A · Hans-Georg Lang
芸能会社

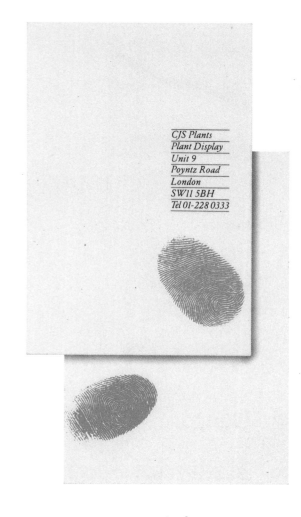

CJS Plants
Plant Display
Unit 9
Poyntz Road
London
SW11 5BH
Tel 01-228 0333

CJS Plants
Office plant displays
England 1983
The Partners (Design Consultants) Ltd.
AD, D · Aziz Cami
オフィス園芸／ディスプレー会社

T

1891 Professional Building
Suite 215
Liberty Square
Danvers / MA   01923

Thoresen and Associates

Thoresen and Associates
Health care company
USA 1985
Laughlin/Winkler
AD, D · Mark Laughlin, Ellen Winkler
健康管理会社

The Type Gallery, Inc.
Typesetting company
USA 1986
Rick Eiber Design
AD, D · Rick Eiber
写植会社

The Type Gallery, Inc.
1121 Westlake Avenue North
Seattle, Washington 98109
Phone (206) 285-6333

Betty Handly
President

S.G. Sriberg
Antique carpets
USA 1988
Laughlin/Winkler
AD, D · Mark Laughlin, Ellen Winkler
アンティーク・カーペット

S.G. Sriberg

205 A Street
Boston/MA
02210

Fort Point Channel

617 268 4012
617 242 9193

By Appointment

Graphic Communication Ltd.

Design firm (business card for the year
of the mouse)

Hong Kong 1984

Graphic Communication Ltd.

AD, D · Henry Steiner

デザイン会社の子年用名刺

Graphic Communication Ltd.

Design firm (business card for the year
of the dog)

Hong Kong 1982

Graphic Communication Ltd.

AD, D · Henry Steiner

デザイン会社の戌年用名刺

Graphic Communication Ltd.

Design firm (business card for the year
of the rooster)

Hong Kong 1981

Graphic Communication Ltd.

AD, D · Henry Steiner

デザイン会社の酉年用名刺

Naj Naj Kozmetika
Cosmetics company
Yugoslavia 1984
Katja Zelinka Škerlavaj
AD, D · Katja Zelinka Škerlavaj
化粧品会社

Naj Naj kozmetika
Kancilja Franc in Marina
Titova 276
61231 Črnuče
Telefon 061/341 950

Naj Naj kozmetika
Titova 276
YU-61231 Črnuče

Naj Naj kozmetika
Titova 276
YU-61231 Črnuče
Telefon 061/341 950

Dangerous Wardrobe
Stylist
USA 1987
Ph. D
AD, D · Michael Hodgson
C · Maria Sarno
スタイリスト

Linda Grewer
Hairdresser
Netherlands 1987
Frans Lieshout
AD, D · Frans Lieshout
美容師

Roselli
Hairstylist
Belgium 1988
Forum Aesthetica Bi
AD, D, A · Michael S.M. Romme,
　Yuko Yoshida
美容師

Chris Blanchard
Photo stylist
USA 1984
Laughlin/Winkler
AD, D · Mark Laughlin, Ellen Winkler
A · Chris Blanchard
フォトスタイリスト

Taboo
Hairdressers
USA 1988
Ph. D
AD, D · Clive Piercy, Michael Hodgson
A · Clive Piercy
美容師

Aprile
Hairdresser
England 1988
Julia Alldridge Associates
AD, D · Julia Alldridge
C · Aprile Farmer
美容師

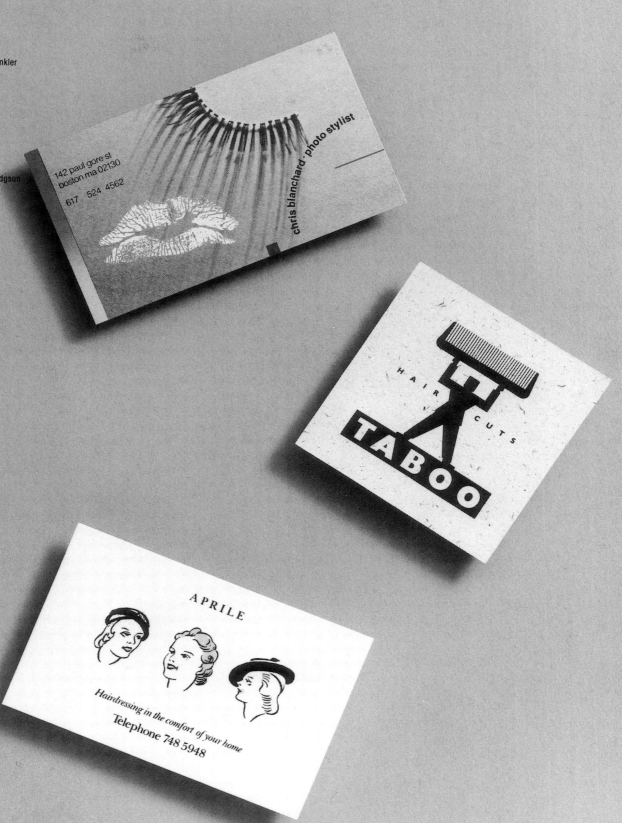

Keiko Hayashi Graphic Design
Graphic designer
USA 1988
Keiko Hayashi Graphic Design
AD, D, A · Keiko Hayashi
グラフィックデザイナー

Reproduction Quality Services
USA
Casado Design
AD, D · John Casado
写真現像所

Tom Lippert
President

Reproduction
Quality Services
10880 Wilshire
Suite 1102
Los Angeles,
California 90024
(213) 474-9532

KEIKO

Playne Design
Furniture, graphic and industrial design
USA 1985
Playne Design
AD, D, A · Debbie Hahn
家具/グラフィック/インダストリアル・デザイン会社

Dean Morris
Graphic designer
USA 1983
Dean Morris Graphic Design
AD, D, A · Dean Morris
グラフィックデザイナー

Playne Design
96 Fort Greene Place
Brooklyn, NY 11217
718 834 8808

Debbie Hahn

Morris
Designer
6 Street
N Y 10003
3 5039

Dean Morris
Graphic Designer
307 East 6 Street
New York N Y 10003
212 533 5039

NEW PHONE
212
420 0673
NUMBER

NEW
D
Grap
307 Ea
New Yor
212 5

Pesca
Cafe-Bar
USA
C · Pesca
カフェ・バー

Franca Emmepi
Italy
C · Franca Emmepi
業種不明

MICHAEL GOSNEY
PUBLISHER

4620 PANORAMA DRIVE, LA MESA, CA 92041   619/463-9977   MCI: VERBUM

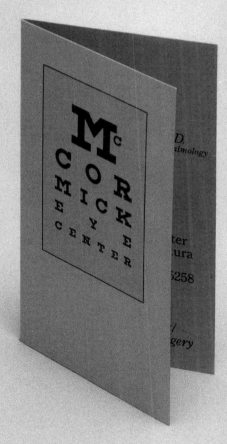

Kangas Design Associates
Industrial design firm
Canada
C · Kangas Design Associates
インダストリアルデザイン会社

Verbum
Personal computer journal
Canada
C · Verbum
パソコン・ジャーナル

McCormick Eye Center
USA
C · McCormick Eye Center
眼科医

Radio Ranch
Music production
USA
AD, D · Woody Pirtle
音楽プロダクション

Zimmer Smith
Music production
USA
AD, D · Woody Pirtle
音楽プロダクション

The Nature Company
Store specialized in natural science
utencils
USA
C · The Nature Company
自然科学関係器物販売店

THE NATURE COMPANY
10250 SANTA MONICA BOULEVARD
LOS ANGELES, CALIFORNIA 90067
213-785-0262

GEO
Landscape and construction
USA 1984
GEO
AD, D · Judy Von Euer
環境設計会社

Summerford Design, Inc.
Graphic design firm
USA 1988
Summerford Design, Inc.
AD, D, A · Jack Summerford
グラフィックデザイン会社

Ca Bianca
Switzerland 1985
Gottschalk + Ash International
AD · Gottschalk + Ash International
D · Fritz Gottschalk
業種不明

Ferny Glen Arabians
Arabian horse stud
Australia 1988
Barrie Tucker Design
AD · Barrie Tucker
D · Barrie Tucker, Nicola Lloyd,
    Catherine Lloyd
A · Nicola Lloyd, Catherine Noel
アラビア馬飼育場

Kessels Upholstering Ltd.
Fine upholstery
Canada 1988
Neville Smith Graphic Design
AD, D, A · Neville Smith
高級家具店

Bonella
Manufacturer of silk scarves
USA 1988
Madeleine Corson Design
AD, D · Madeleine Corson
A · Eric Hulob
シルク・スカーフ会社

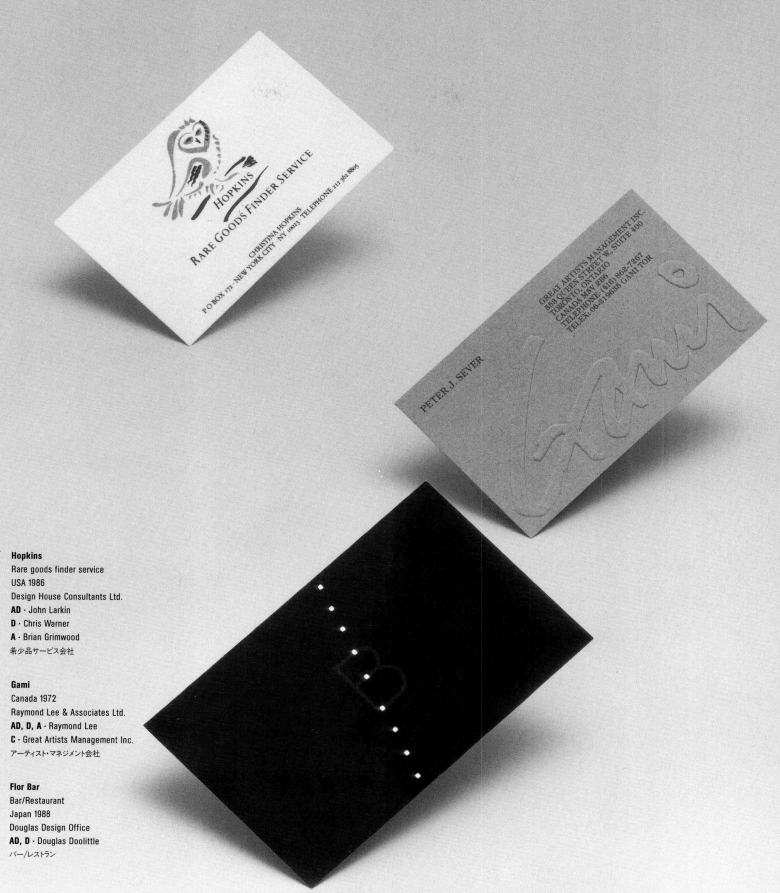

Hopkins
Rare goods finder service
USA 1986
Design House Consultants Ltd.
AD · John Larkin
D · Chris Warner
A · Brian Grimwood
希少品サービス会社

Gami
Canada 1972
Raymond Lee & Associates Ltd.
AD, D, A · Raymond Lee
C · Great Artists Management Inc.
アーティスト・マネジメント会社

Flor Bar
Bar/Restaurant
Japan 1988
Douglas Design Office
AD, D · Douglas Doolittle
バー/レストラン

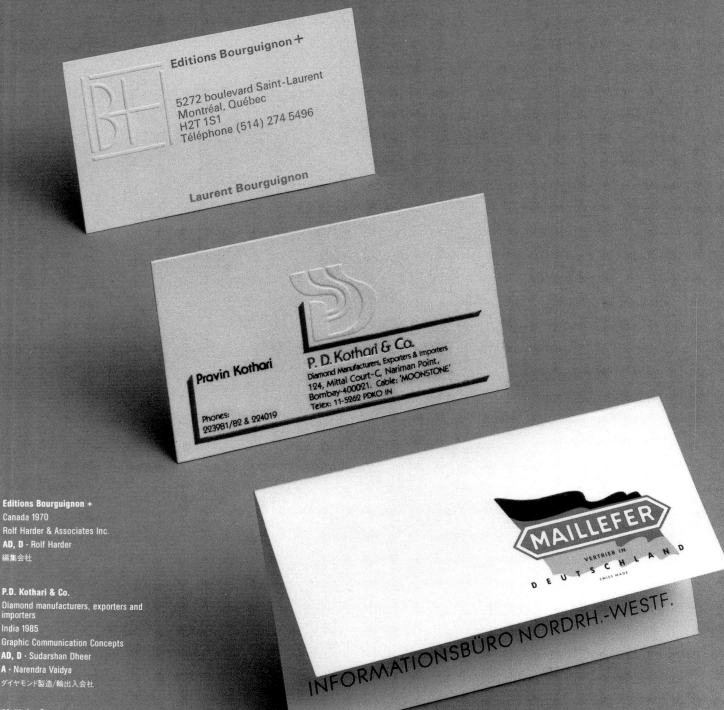

Editions Bourguignon +
Canada 1970
Rolf Harder & Associates Inc.
AD, D · Rolf Harder
編集会社

P.D. Kothari & Co.
Diamond manufacturers, exporters and importers
India 1985
Graphic Communication Concepts
AD, D · Sudarshan Dheer
A · Narendra Vaidya
ダイヤモンド製造/輸出入会社

Maillefer Germany
Dental instruments distributor
West Germany 1988
Lang Art + Graphic-Design
AD, D, A · Hans-Georg Lang
歯科医療具販売業

CORPORACION CIMEX S.A.
Carlos Alfonso
Presidente

Apartado 63876
El Dorado
República de Panamá
Teléfono 267235-36
Telex: 2385 PANATEX

Calle 8 Número 303
Esq. a 3ra. Miramar
Habana, Cuba
Teléfono 20 5921
Telex 511269 CIMEX

Winters & Associates
P.O. Box 278
Yokohama Port Post Office
Yokohama 231-91, Japan
Telephone 641-0802
Cable "Skyway Yokohama"

Charlie Winters
President

Winters & Associates
P.O. Box 278
Yokohama Port Post Offi
Yokohama 231-91, Japa
Telephone 641-0802
Cable "Skyway Yokoham

Wataru Sakai
Vice President Sales

Corporación Cimex S.A.
Importer
Mexico 1979
Félix Beltrán & Associates
AD, D, A · Félix Beltrán
貿易会社

Winters + Associates
Sales representative
Japan 1975
Richard Moore Associates
AD, D · Richard Moore
販売代理業

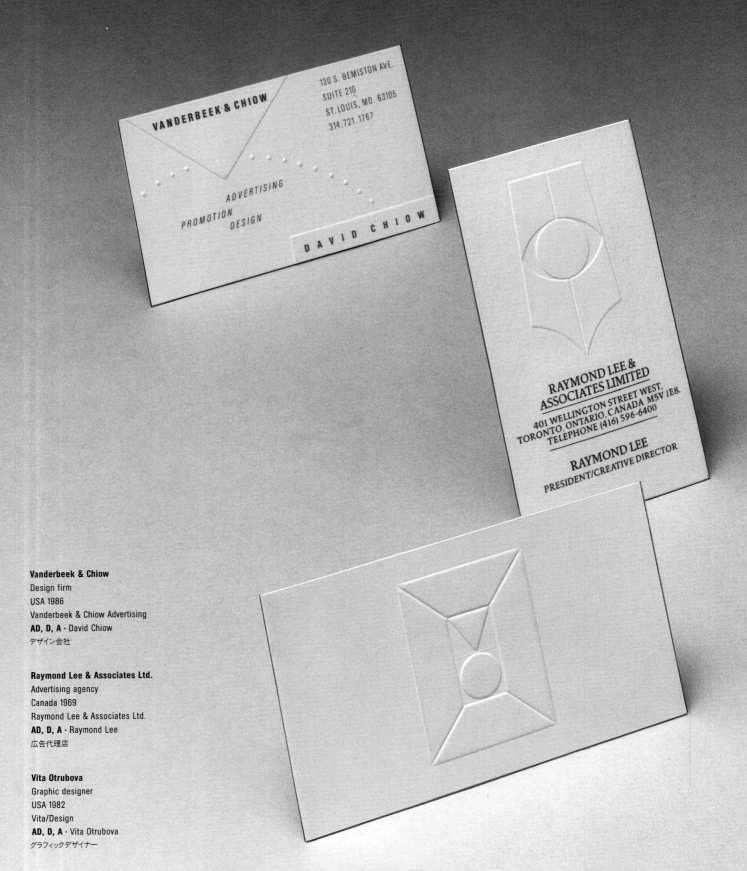

VANDERBEEK & CHIOW

130 S. BEMISTON AVE.
SUITE 210
ST. LOUIS, MO. 63105
314.721.1767

ADVERTISING
PROMOTION DESIGN

DAVID CHIOW

RAYMOND LEE &
ASSOCIATES LIMITED
401 WELLINGTON STREET WEST,
TORONTO, ONTARIO, CANADA M5V 1E8,
TELEPHONE (416) 596-6400

RAYMOND LEE
PRESIDENT/CREATIVE DIRECTOR

Vanderbeek & Chiow
Design firm
USA 1986
Vanderbeek & Chiow Advertising
AD, D, A · David Chiow
デザイン会社

Raymond Lee & Associates Ltd.
Advertising agency
Canada 1969
Raymond Lee & Associates Ltd.
AD, D, A · Raymond Lee
広告代理店

Vita Otrubova
Graphic designer
USA 1982
Vita/Design
AD, D, A · Vita Otrubova
グラフィックデザイナー

Kijuro Yahagi
Graphic designer
Japan 1988
Kijuro Yahagi
AD, D, A · Kijuro Yahagi
グラフィックデザイナー

The Weller Institute for the Cure of Design, Inc.
Graphic design firm
USA 1985
The Weller Institute for the Cure of Design, Inc.
AD, D, A · Don Weller
グラフィックデザイン会社

Arnold Schwartzman
Graphic designer
England 1970
Arnold Schwartzman Productions, Inc.
AD, D, A · Arnold Schwartzman
グラフィックデザイナー

The Research Business
Market research group
Australia 1986
Collide Pty. Ltd.
AD, D, A · Clyde Terry
マーケット・リサーチ会社

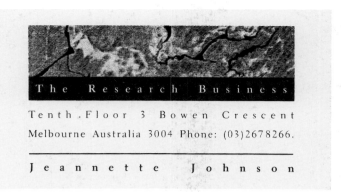

Thomas Spencer and Associates
Personal financial planning
Hong Kong
Kenyon Ltd.
AD, D · Elizabeth Kenyon
金融業

Turner Spurrier Ltd.
Public relations firm
Hong Kong 1987
Graphic Communication Ltd.
AD, D · Henry Steiner
PR 会社

TONY TURNER
Director

Public Affairs, Financial and Marketing Communication

Turner Spurrier Limited *2-10 Lyndhurst Terrace 4/F, Hong Kong*
Telephone 5-438882 Facsimile 5-433030 Telex 82840 TSPUR

Myrna Davis
Writer
USA 1984
Paul Davis Studio
AD · Paul Davis
D · Jose Conde
執筆家

Interlinx Marketing
USA 1988
Rod Dyer Group Inc.
AD · Rod Dyer
D · Harriet Baba
C · Kathy Kompaniez
マーケティング・コンサルタント会社

Personal Financial progress, Inc.
Personal financial managment
USA 1973
The Weller Institute for the Cure of
Design, Inc.
AD, D, A · Don Weller
金融業

Food Art & Design C
Food stylist
Japan 1987
Igarashi Studio
AD · Takenobu Igarashi
D · Noreen Fukumori, Honami Morita
C · Masaki Samejima
フード・スタイリスト

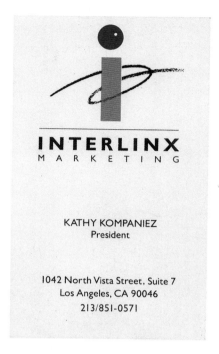

Heaven
Retail store
USA
Dyer/Kahn, Inc.
D · Vantan
小売店

The Group Advertising Ltd.
Hong Kong 1983
Kan Tai-keung Design & Associates Ltd.
AD, D · Kan Tai-keung
広告会社

Vertigo
Clothing and accessories
USA 1979
April Greiman Inc.
AD, D · April Greiman
衣料/アクセサリー

R. Fox Limited
Exhibition contractors
England 1976
Minale, Tattersfield and Partners Ltd.
AD, D, A · Alex Maranzano
催事設備会社

Eureka! The Children's Museum Ltd.
Education center for children
England 1987
Pentagram Design Ltd.
AD · Mervyn Kurlansky
D · Mervyn Kurlansky, Claire Johnson
A · N/A
児童教育センター

Giscal, Hair & Make-up
Italy 1988
Studio "Visual Due"
AD, D · Vittorio Prina
美容院

Tim Girvin Design, Inc.   911 Western Avenue   206 623 7808
Suite 408   206 623 7918
Seattle, WA 98104-1031

Telecopier number
206 340 1837

RICK   EIBER   DESIGN

3019 Northwest 65th   4649 Sunnyside N.
Seattle, WA. 98107   Seattle, WA. 98103

Home   *Studio*
(206) 782-7647   (206) 632-8326

Rick Eiber

R   E   D

Tim Girvin Design
Graphic designer
USA 1982
Tim Girvin Design
AD, D, A · Tim Girvin
グラフィックデザイナー

Red
Graphic design firm
USA 1985
Rick Eiber Design
AD, D · Rick Eiber
グラフィックデザイン会社

Wohnflex
Design furniture shop
Switzerland 1984
BBV
AD, D · Michael Baviera
デザイン家具店

WOHNFLEX
Beim Römerhof

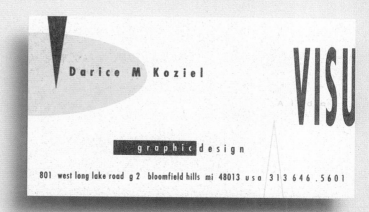

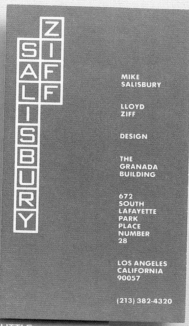

DOUGLAS DOOLITTLE
ダグラス ドリトル

DOUGLAS DESIGN OFFICE
Shibuya-ku, Kamiyama-cho, 12-7,
#201 Uchino Heights, Tokyo, Japan, 〒150
Tel. (03) 467-5996   Fax (03) 466-8446

ダグラスデザイン事務所
〒150 東京都渋谷区神山町12-7
内野ハイツ201号
電話 (03) 467-5996 ファックス (03) 466-8446

Darice M. Koziel
Graphic designer
USA 1988
Cranbrook Academy of Art
AD · Katherine McCoy
D · Darice M. Koziel
グラフィックデザイナー

Ziff Salisbury
Graphic design firm
USA
Ziff Salisbury Design
AD, D · Salisbury Design
グラフィックデザイン会社

Douglas Design Office
Graphic design firm
Japan 1985
Douglas Design Office
AD, D · Douglas Doolittle
グラフィックデザイン会社

Judit Muller Design
Graphic designer
USA 1988
Gillian/Craig Associates
AD, D · Judit Muller
グラフィックデザイナー

Weisz Yang Dunkelberger Inc.
Graphic design firm
USA 1984
Weisz Yang Dunkelberger Inc.
AD, D · Larry Yang
グラフィックデザイン会社

Graphic Communication Ltd.
Design firm (business card
for the year of the horse)
Hong Kong 1978
Graphic Communication Ltd.
AD, D · Henry Steiner
デザイン会社の午年用名刺

Vanderbyl Design
Graphic design firm
USA
Vanderbyl Design
AD, D · Michael Vanderbyl
グラフィックデザイン会社

Laughlin/Winkler
Design firm
USA 1981
Laughlin/Winkler
AD, D · Mark Laughlin, Ellen Winkler
デザイン会社

Jonathan Louie
Graphic designer
USA
C · Jonathan Louie
グラフィックデザイナー

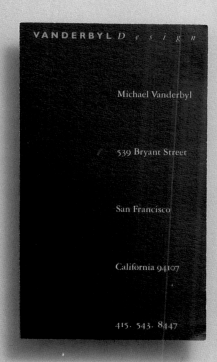

THE KENWOOD GROUP

IMPRINTS

40 GRANT AVE

SAN FRANCISCO CA

9 4 1 0 8

415 788 0747

Executive Producer

One China Basin
Building
San Francisco
California 94107
415 777 5777

SINCE 1987

San Francisco's first authentic

Singapore Restaurant

3815 Geary Boulevard
San Francisco
California 94117
415 668 1783

STRAITS CAFE

OZZIE'S DELI

Delicatessen, Breakfast,
Lunch & Catering

1500 El Camino Real
Belmont, Ca 94002
594-1974

Straits Cafe
Singapore restaurant
USA 1987
The Design Office of Wong & Yeo
AD, D, A · Hock Wah Yeo
レストラン

Imprints
Poster/Print store
USA 1985
The Design Office of Wong & Yeo
AD, D, A · Valerie Wong
ポスター/印刷物販売店

The Kenwood Group
Film/Video production company
USA
The Design Office of Wong & Yeo
AD, D, A · Hock Wah Yeo
映画/ビデオ製作会社

Ozzie's Deli
Catering service
USA 1988
The Design Office of Wong & Yeo
AD, D, A · Valerie Wong
ケイタリング・サービス

Collide Design
Design firm
Australia 1986
Collide Pty. Ltd.
AD, D · Clyde Terry
A · Collide + Bits
デザイン会社

Four In Hand
Bar & Restaurant
Australia 1987
Annette Harcus Design
AD, D, A · Annette Harcus
C · Valdis Gravelis
バー/レストラン

Fountain Court
USA 1986
Sussman/Prejza + Co.
AD · Deborah Sussman
D · Vince Peterson, John Temple
業種不明

V A T U L E L E

18°30' South 177°37' East

VILLAGE VINTNER,
WINE NEGOCIANTS
AND PURVEYORS
OF FINE WINES
AND SPIRITS

MARINE VILLAGE
SANCTUARY COVE
RESORT, HOPE ISLAND
QUEENSLAND 4212
PHONE (075) 308400

Vatulele Island Resort
Australia 1988
Flett Henderson & Arnold
AD · Richard Henderson
D, A · Flett Henderson & Arnold
リゾート施設

Village Vintner
Premium wine shop
Australia 1987
Barrie Tucker Design
AD · Barrie Tucker
D · Barrie Tucker, Elizabeth Schlooz
A · Elizabeth Schlooz
C · Sanctuary Cove Resort
ワイン・ショップ

Clips
Photographic and graphic arts
representatives
Brazil 1978
Ao Lapis Studio (Animus Propaganda)
AD · Rique Nitzsche
D · Rique Nitzsche, Roberto Renner
A · Roberto Renner
写真家/グラフィックデザイナーの代理業

Fotografia, Cinema
e Artes Gráficas

Clips

Representantes:

Rio: Luz e Sombra
Shopping Center da Gávea
Rua Marquês de São Vicente 52 / L: 202
Telefone: 274 9096

São Paulo: Adriana Beretta
Rua Clodomiro Amazonas 67 / C: 2
Itaím / Telefone: 64 2858

Andy Allen
Cosmetologist
USA 1988
Timothy Hartford
AD, D · Timothy Hartford
美容師

Fuego Films
Film company
Spain 1984
Medina Design
AD, D · Fernando Medina
映画会社

Savage Friedman Inc.
Film production company
USA 1968
Milton Glaser, Inc.
AD, D, A · Milton Glaser
C · Harold Friedman
映画製作会社

VELAZQUEZ 160
Telfs. 411 60 43 - 411 61 47
MADRID 6

Harold Friedman

ZUNI
Cafe & Grill
ZUNI   1658 Market Street
            San Francisco 94102
            415 552-2522

Bronx Bar
Bar
Japan 1988
Douglas Design Office
AD, D · Douglas Doolittle
バー

Zuni
Restaurant
USA 1982
Carron Design
AD · Ross Carron
D · Ross Carron, Peter Soe
レストラン

Tortola
Restaurant
USA 1986
Carron Design
AD, D · Ross Carron
A · Judith Tan
レストラン

Mind Co.,Ltd.
Restaurant operation and planning
company
Japan 1987
Douglas Design Office
AD, D · Douglas Doolittle
レストラン経営/プランニング会社

Tyler Trafficante
Fashion boutique
USA 1989
Ph.D
AD, D · Clive Piercy, Michael Hodgson
ファッション・ブティック

Shimokochi/Reeves Design
Graphic design firm
USA 1988
Shimokochi/Reeves Design
AD · Mamoru Shimokochi, Anne Reeves
D · Mamoru Shimokochi, Kathryn Walker
グラフィックデザイン会社

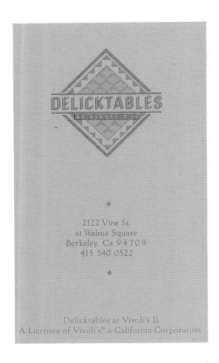

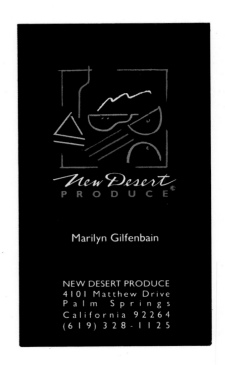

Delicktables
Confectionery store
USA 1985
The Design Office of Wong & Yeo
AD, D, A · Valerie Wong
菓子店

Spuntino
Restaurant
USA 1986
Ph.D
AD, D, A · Clive Piercy
C · Spectrum Foods
レストラン

New Desert Produce
Produce company
USA 1986
Ph.D
AD, D, A · Clive Piercy
企画開発会社

Pane e Vino Trattoria
Restaurant
USA
Rod Dyer Group Inc.
AD, D, A · Rod Dyer
レストラン

Jolimont Cellars
Winery and cellars
Australia 1987
Annette Harcus Design
AD, D · Annette Harcus
A · Annette Harcus, Melinda Dudley
C · ICM Australia — Anabel Carter
ワイン会社

1482 E. Valley Road
Santa Barbara
California 93108
(805) 969-9274

JOLIMONT WINES PTY. LTD.
Jolimont Cellars
Drummond Street · Rutherglen
Victoria 3685

Telephone (060) 32 9922
Facsimile (060) 32 9030

Piramida
Pizzeria
Yugoslavia 1987
Studio KROG
AD, D · Edi Berk
C · Živojin Vladović
ピザ店

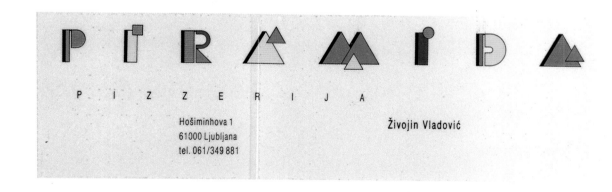

PIZZERIJA

Hošiminhova 1
61000 Ljubljana
tel. 061/349 881

Živojin Vladović

The Slide Gallery
Slide company
USA 1986
Rick Eiber Design
AD, D · Rick Eiber
スライド会社

Jean yates
USA
C · Jean yates
業種不明

Kan Tai-keung Design & Associates
Graphic design firm
Hong Kong 1988
Kan Tai-keung Design & Associates Ltd.
AD · Kan Tai-keung
D · Kan Tai-keung, Eddy Yu
グラフィックデザイン会社

Caroline Film Limited
Film company
England 1964
Minale, Tattersfield and Partners Ltd.
AD, D, A · Marcello Minale,
　　Brian Tattersfield
映画会社

Nob + Non Utsumi
USA
C · Nob + Non Utsumi
業種不明

Sally North Beauchamp

CarolineFilm Limited 2 Charles Street Berkeley Square London W1 Mayfair 6751

Nob+Non Utsumi • 300 East 59th Street • Suite 3004 • New York, NY 10022 • Phone 688-4835

Helburn
TV director
USA 1982
Federico Design
AD, D · Gene Federico
C · William Helburn Productions Ltd.
テレビ・ディレクター

Toni Ficalora
Photographer
USA 1969
Federico Design
AD, D · Gene Federico
写真家

Ruth Raible
Craft and folk art gallery and dealer
USA 1987
Steff Geissbuhler
AD, D, A · Steff Geissbuhler
工芸品/民芸品展示販売業

Recto-Recto
France 1978
Grapus
AD, D, A · Grapus
業種不明

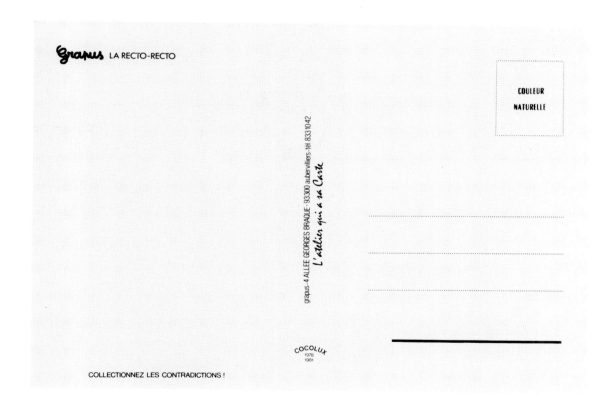

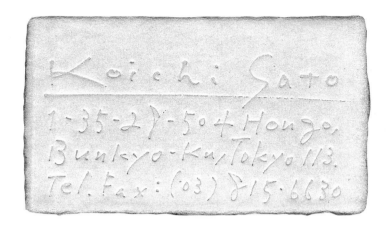

Koichi Sato
1-35-2Y-504 Hongo,
Bunkyo-ku, Tokyo 113.
Tel. Fax : (03) 815·6630

APE inc.

President Director
Shigesato ITOI

6F, Minami Aoyama Daiichi Mansion 602
5-1-10, Minami Aoyama, Minato-ku, Tokyo 107, Japan,
TEL.03-5485-2553 FAX.03-400-7372

Rikiya Yasuoka

岡
安
カ也

WARNER PIONEER CO.LTD.
14F New Aoyama Building East
1-1-1 Minami Aoyama Minato-ku Tokyo Japan
TELEPHONE 03(475)2064

吉本一平

〒一〇六
東京都港区西麻布三十一·二十九《小山ビル》
電·〇三·四七五·四〇四一

てうち
そろり

Koichi Sato
Graphic designer
Japan 1989
Koichi Sato Design Studio
AD, D · Sato Koichi
グラフィックデザイナー

Ape Inc.
Computer game software company
Japan 1988
Asaba Design Co., ltd.
AD, D · Masaharu Takada
コンピュータ・ゲームソフト会社

Rikiya Yasuoka
Singer
Japan 1985
K-Two Co., Ltd.
AD, D · Seitaro Kuroda
D · Masayuki Takahashi
C · Yuya Uchida, Warner Pioneer Co., Ltd.
歌手

Sorori
Japanese noodle restaurant
Japan 1987
Koichi Sato Design Studio
AD, D · Koichi Sato
うどん屋

Catherine Zask & Kenji
Graphic designers
France 1988
Catherine Zask & Kenji
AD, D, A · Catherine Zask & Kenji
グラフィックデザイナー

Catherine Zask
Graphic designer
France 1986/88
AD, D, A · Catherine Zask
グラフィックデザイナー

Catherine Zask
Graphic designer
France 1986/88
Catherine Zask
AD, D, A · Catherine Zask
グラフィックデザイナー

R O X Y

PRODUCTIONS

PTY LTD

RAY WAGSTAFF
DIRECTOR

288 COVENTRY ST

STH MELBOURNE

AUSTRALIA 3205

PHONE (03) 690 2364

TELEX CAMFIL 37688

THE DEMANN ENTERTAINMENT COMPANY

Neysa DeMann

9200 Sunset Boulevard Suite 915

Los Angeles California 90069

213 550 8181 Telex 277824 DeMann

RIVER FILMS

PHIL AGLAND

HALE DAIRY FARM

HALE *near* FORDINGBRIDGE

HAMPSHIRE SP6 2RG

TELEPHONE (0725) 22159

Roxy Productions
TV & Film production company
Australia 1985
Condon Payne Terry Pty. Ltd.
AD, D, A · CPT
テレビ/映画製作会社

The DeMann Entertainment Company
USA 1987
Vigon Seireeni
AD, D, A · Vigon Seireeni
芸能会社

River Films
Film production company
England 1988
The Partners (Design Consultants) Ltd.
AD · Stephen Gibbons
D · David Kimpton
映画製作会社

At Close Range
Film production company
USA 1986
Ph.D
AD, D · Michael Hodgson
A · Reynolds Stone
C · Hemdale Releasing Corp.
映画製作会社

Hans Groenwold
Film production company
Netherlands 1987
Frans Lieshout
AD, D · Frans Lieshout
映画製作会社

Healing Arts Home Video
Video production company
USA 1986
Shimokochi/Reeves Design
AD · Mamoru Shimokochi, Anne Reeves
D · Mamoru Shimokochi
ビデオ製作会社

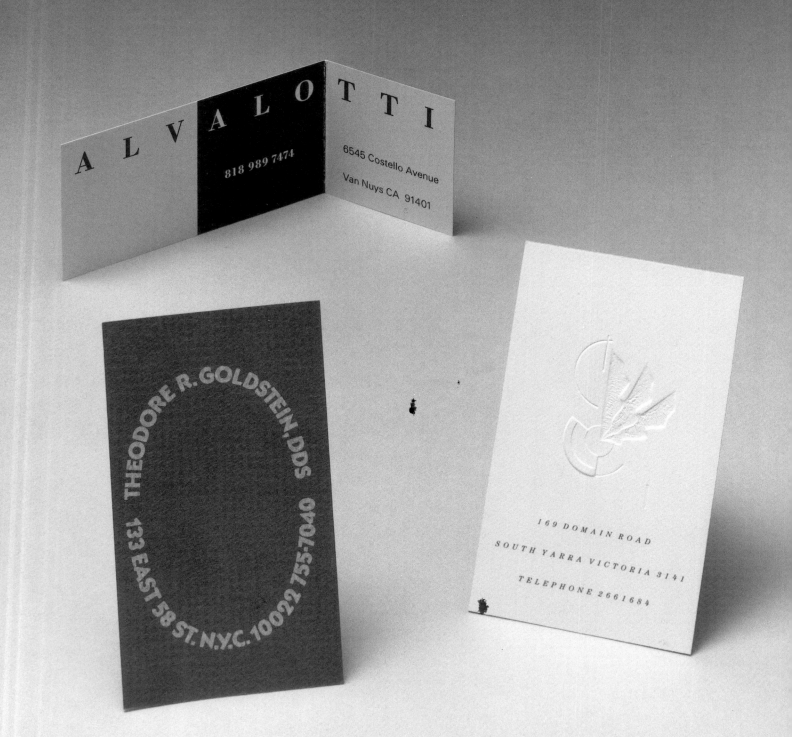

Alvalotti
Interior design studio
USA 1987
Luci Goodman Studio
AD, D, · Luci Goodman
インテリアデザイン・スタジオ

Theodore Goldstein, DDS
Dentist
USA 1974
David Leigh
AD, D, A · David Leigh
歯科医師

Botanical Hotel
Australia 1987
Emery Vincent Associates
AD, D, A · Emery Vincent Associates
ホテル

Novara Holdings Inc.
Importers of Italian goods
Canada 1984
Neville Smith Graphic Design
AD, D, A · Neville Smith
イタリア製品輸入会社

Sylvie Delézay
France
Catherine Zask
AD, D · Catherine Zask
業種不明

V.J. Pagliaro

NOVARA
Novara Holdings Incorporated, 231 MacKay Street,
Ottawa, Ontario, Canada K1M 2B6 (613) 745-3939

SYLVIE DELÉZAY

ÉTUDES ET RECHERCHES EN COMMUNICATION
4, AV. LAMARTINE 94170 LE PERREUX/MARNE. 43 24 54 20

SYLVIE DELÉZAY

ÉTUDES ET RECHERCHES
EN COMMUNICATION
4, AVENUE LAMARTINE
94170 LE PERREUX/MARNE.
43 24 54 20

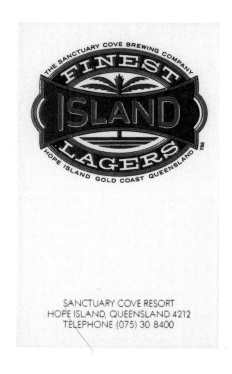

Tilley Consulting Group Pty. Ltd.
Consulting engineers/Interior designers
Australia 1988
Cozzolino/Ellett Design D'Vision
AD · Mimmo Cozzolino
D · Philip Ellett
A · Diane Monks
インテリアデザイン会社

Craig Foster-Lynam
Illustrator/Designer
Australia 1988
Craig Foster-Lynam Illustration & Design
AD, D, A · Craig Foster-Lynam
イラストレーター/デザイナー

Sanctuary Cove Brewing Company
Australia 1987
Barrie Tucker Design
AD · Barrie Tucker
D · Barrie Tucker, Elizabeth Schlooz
A · Elizabeth Schlooz
C · Sanctuary Cove Resort
ビール会社

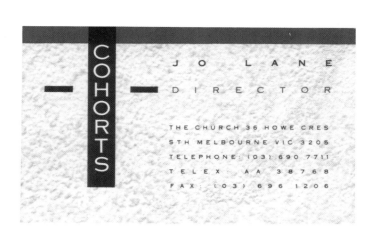

Cohorts

TV/Film production company

Australia 1988

Condon Payne Terry Pty. Ltd.

AD, D, A · CPT

テレビ/映画製作会社

The Anchorage

Waterfront restaurant

West Indies 1988

Russel Halfhide Graphic Design

AD, D, A · Russel Halfhide

レストラン

Kokusai Sake Kai

Sake association

USA 1987

UCI Inc./Urano Communication International

AD · Ryo Urano

D, A · Dan Sato

日本酒協会

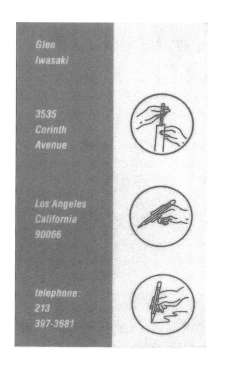

R.T. Jones Capital Equities, Inc.
USA 1987
Vanderbeek & Chiow Advertising
AD, D, A · David Chiow
投資会社

Glen Iwasaki
Graphic designer
USA
N.F.L. Properties, Inc.
AD, D · Glen Iwasaki
グラフィックデザイナー

Bal-Bar
Bar
Japan 1988
Douglas Design Office
AD, D · Douglas Doolittle
バー

Knit Design
Knit wear fashion designer
USA 1987
Noreen Rei Fukumori
AD, D · Noreen Rei Fukumori
C · Bettina Žurek
ニット・ファッション・デザイナー

Alan Chan Design Co.
Graphic design firm
Hong Kong 1988
Alan Chan Design Co.
AD, D · Alan Chan
グラフィックデザイン会社

Wolf Dietrich Jurck und Partner
Architectural company
West Germany 1984
Minale, Tattersfield and Partners Ltd.
AD, D, A · Brian Tattersfield
建築設計会社

Wides Photography
Photographer
USA 1984
Tenazaz Design
AD, D, A · Lucille Tenazas
C · Susan Wides
写真家

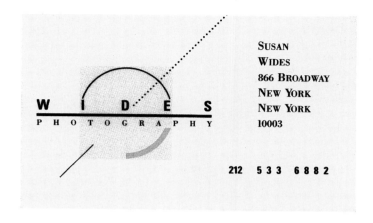

Precarn Associates Inc.
Technologies research consortia
Canada 1987
Rushton, Green and Grossutti Inc.
AD · Keith Rushton, Marcello Grossutti
D · Margaret Crewe
技術リサーチ協会

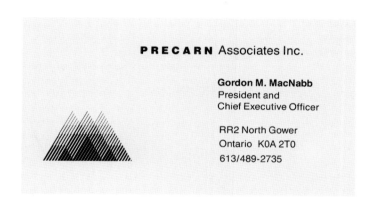

Ralph Mercer
Photographer
USA 1984
Laughlin/Winkler
AD, D · Mark Laughlin, Ellen Winkler
写真家

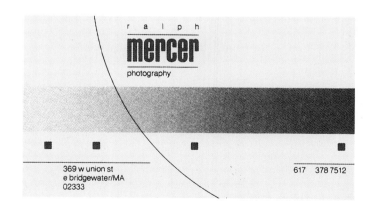

Carlos Navajas
Photographer
Spain 1984
Medina Design
AD, D, A · Fernando Medina
写真家

Carlos Navajas
Fotógrafo
Vinaroz 16-B-3-11
28002 Madrid Spain
Tel. 415 50 35

Marco Pirovano
Photographer
Italy 1987
Studio "Visual Due"
AD, D, A · Vittorio Prina
写真家

20133 Milano Via F. Reina, 24 Tel: 02. 7386928 **Marco Pirovano**

Anil Dave
Photographer
India 1982
Graphic Communication Concepts
AD, D · Sudarshan Dheer
A · Prakash Patil
写真家

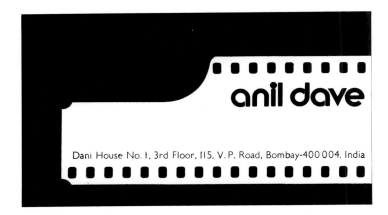

anil dave

Dani House No. 1, 3rd Floor, 115, V. P. Road, Bombay-400 004. India

Majeed A.A.
Graphic designer
India 1980
Majeed A.A.
AD, D, A · Majeed A.A.
グラフィックデザイナー

Anita Meyer
Graphic designer
USA 1985
Anita Meyer Design
AD, D · Anita Meyer
A · N.A.
グラフィックデザイナー

■ **Anita Meyer** Graphic Design

● 10 Thatcher Street
Suite 509
Boston, Massachusetts 02113
Tel 617.367.9587
Fax 617.720.2373

Udo Schliemann
Graphic designer
West Germany 1986
Udo Schliemann
AD, D · Udo Schliemann
グラフィックデザイナー

Udo Schliemann

Grafik-Design
Am Kriegsbergturm 41
7000 Stuttgart 1
Tel. 0711/2571469

Eric Read
Graphic designer
USA 1988
Read + Associates
AD, D, A · Eric Read
グラフィックデザイナー

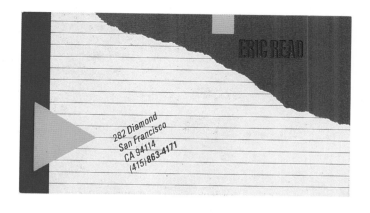

Allan Wyatt Pty. Ltd.
Landscape architects
Australia 1985
Emery Vincent Associates
AD, D, A · Emery Vincent Associates
環境設計会社

Mascot Developments Ltd.
Property development company
England 1984
W M de Majo Associates
AD · W M de Majo
D · W M de Majo MBE FCSD
A · John Eason MCSD
不動産開発会社

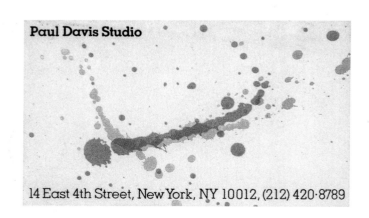

Paul Davis Studio
Illustrator
USA 1984
Paul Davis Studio
AD · Paul Davis
D · Paul Davis, José Conde
イラストレーター

FM 802
Broadcasting station
Japan 1988
K-Two Co., Ltd.
AD · Keisuke Nagatomo
D · Kazumi Urushibata
A · Seitaro Kuroda
C · FM 802
放送局

U.G. Sato
Graphic designer
Japan 1984
U.G. Sato & Design Farm
AD, D, A · U.G. Sato
グラフィックデザイナー

U-Meta Design, Inc.
Industrial/Interior design firm
Japan 1986
PAOS, Inc.
AD, D · PAOS, Inc.
インダストリアル/インテリア・デザイン会社

Barrie Tucker Design
Graphic design consultancy
Australia 1987
Barrie Tucker Design
AD, D, · Barrie Tucker
A · Mark Janetzki
グラフィックデザイン・コンサルタント会社

Ernest T. Nagamatsu
Dentist
USA
Ernest T. Nagamatsu, D.D.S., Inc.
AD, D · Ernest T. Nagamatsu
A · Colleen Hendrickson
歯科医師

Pamon Gonzalez Teja
Illustrator
Spain 1980
Medina Disign
AD, D · Fernando Medina
イラストレーター

EDDIE JURKIEWICZ
Managing Partner

CONVERGENT
DESIGN

Convergent Design
Associates Pty. Ltd.
Unit 1, Node 375
11 Brodie Hall Drive
Bentley 6102
Western Australia
Tel: (09) 470 3411
Telex: AA96824
Fax: (09) 470 3985

OLSON
SUNDBERG
ARCHITECTS

Jim Olson
Architect

1507 Western Avenue
Seattle, WA 98101
206.624.5670

Yukie Namiki
Product Development Division

OUN Corporation
Seventh Minami Aoyama Bldg.
7-12-14 Minami Aoyama
Minato-ku, Tokyo 107 Japan
Tel 03-486-1011/Fax 03-486-1900
Telex J27495 OUNTKY

Convergent Design
Design firm
Australia 1988
Rick Lambert Design Consultants
AD, D · Rick Lambert
A · Rick Lambert, Katherine Mogan
デザイン会社

Olson/Sundberg
Architectual firm
USA 1987
Tim Girvin Design
AD, D · Tim Girvin
建築設計会社

OUN International Ltd.
Design firm
Japan 1987
Igarashi Studio
AD · Takenobu Igarashi
D · Debi Shimamoto
デザイン会社

Metro Cafe
Restaurant
USA 1986
LaPine/O'Very
AD, D, A · Julia LaPine
レストラン

Record
Publishing company
Australia 1988
Condon Payne Terry
AD, D · CPT
D · Clyde Terry
C · Lisa Walton
出版社

Dragon Holdings International Ltd.
Holding company
Hong Kong 1988
Kan Tai-keung Design & Associates Ltd.
AD · Kan Tai-keung
D · Freeman Lau
持株会社

Alma
Representative
Brazil 1988
Animus Propaganda
AD · Rique Nitzsche
D · Rique Nitzsche, Gisela Fiúza
A · Rique Nitzsche, Joaō Simoēs Lopes
権利交渉代理業

Sam Williams
M E T R O   C A F E
39 Post Office Place   Salt Lake City, Utah 84101   (801) 532-2226

REAL ESTATE RECORD

Lisa Walton Publisher

117 VICTORIA AVENUE
ALBERT PARK 3206
PHONE: (03) 696 4499

Dragon Holdings International Ltd.
21st Floor, Hang Lung Bank Building
8 Hysan Avenue, Causeway Bay
Hong Kong
Telephone: 5-766698
Facsimile: 5-774174

Dr. Frank W.K. Chan
B.A.Sc., M.B.A., L.H.D. (Hon.)
Chairman

Beatriz de Kossmann Nitzsche

ALMA
REPRESENTAÇÕES LTDA.

Ladeira do Ascurra, 115 A/Cosme Velho/22241/Rio/Brasil
Telefone: (021) 285 7054/Telex: (021) 22069/APAC

Jardines
Estate agent
England 1988
Lloyd Northover Ltd.
AD · Linda Loe
D · Simon Neale
不動産仲介業

Jan Terrell

JARDINES

18 Culver Road, Winchester
Hampshire SO23 9JF England
Tel: 0962 64129, Fax: 0962 54724

Hasbro, Inc.
USA 1987
Sussman/Prejza
AD, D · Deborah Sussman
業種不明

HASBRO

Robert C. Hubbell
VICE PRESIDENT
INVESTOR RELATIONS

32 W 23RD ST
NEW YORK NY
10010

TEL **212 645 2400**
FAX 212 645 4055
TELEX 681 4168

HASBRO, INC.

Image
Company selling postcards
and videos on cruiseships
British West Indies 1987
Pentagram Design Ltd.
AD · John Rushworth
D · John Rushworth, Frank Schroeder
A · N/A
C · John Davis
ポストカード/ビデオの卸販売会社

PO Box 1220 Grand Cayman British West Indies Telephone 809 94 95758 Telex 4392 Fax 809 94 97707 IMAGE

Thomas Heiser Photo Studio
USA 1988
Madeleine Corson Design
AD, D · Madeleine Corson
写真スタジオ

M & Co.
Graphic design firm
USA 1985
M & Co.
AD · Tibor Kalman
D · Stephen Doyle
グラフィックデザイン会社

Darien Properties
Real estate management firm
USA 1986
Ross McBride
AD, D, A · Ross McBride
C · Claire A. McBride
不動産管理会社

G. Salchow Design
Graphic design firm
USA 1986
G. Salchow Design
AD, D · Gordon Salchow
グラフィックデザイン会社

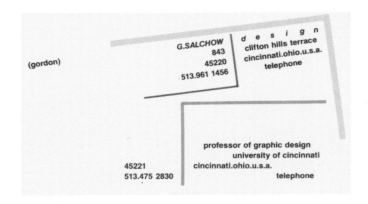

Harry Metzler
Graphic designer
Australia 1986
Harry Metzler Artdesign
AD, D · Harry Metzler
グラフィックデザイナー

David French
Sign painter
USA 1984
The Design Office of Wong & Yeo
AD, D, A · Valerie Wong
看板屋

Personal Best, Inc.
Personal improvement consultants
USA 1988
Gormley/Takei, Inc.
AD, D, A · Koji Takei
個人コンサルタント

Lightplan (Consultants) Ltd.
Lighting consultants
England 1983
Trickett & Webb Ltd.
AD · Cynn Trickett, Brian Webb
D · Marion Dalley, Cynn Trickett,
　 Brian Webb
照明コンサルタント

Palm Press
Greeting card company
USA 1987
Noreen Rei Fukumori
AD, D, A · Noreen Rei Fukumori
グリーティングカード会社

Katsuhiko Hibino
Artist
Japan 1989
Hibino Special
AD, D, A · Katsuhiko Hibino
アーティスト

Galerie Agnés B
Art gallery
Japan 1989
Hibino Special
AD, D, A · Katsuhiko Hibino
アート・ギャラリー

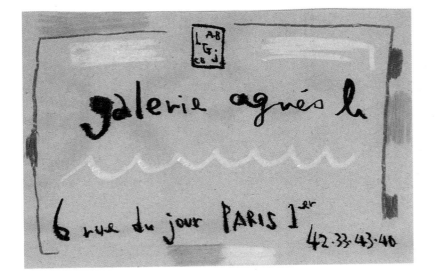

Nissu Art
Manufacturer of stainless steel products
Japan 1989
NDC Graphics
AD · Kenzo Nakagawa
D · Kenzo Nakagawa, Hiroyasu Nobuyama
ステンレス製品会社

Eff Open Systems Co., Ltd.
Planning/Editorial firm
Japan 1974
PAOS, Inc.
AD, D · PAOS, Inc.
企画/編集会社

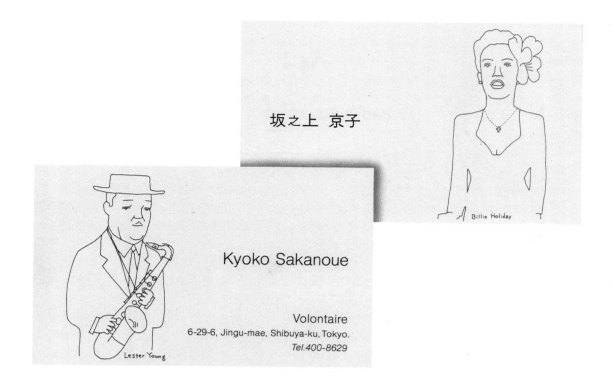

坂之上 京子

Billie Holiday

Kyoko Sakanoue

Volontaire
6-29-6, Jingu-mae, Shibuya-ku, Tokyo.
Tel.400-8629

Lester Young

Volontaire
Bar
Japan 1987
Kojitani, Irie & Inc.
AD · Hiroshi Kojitani
D · Kensuke Irie
A · Makoto Wada
バー

Office "B"
Planning company
Japan 1987
K-Two Co., Ltd.
AD · Keisuke Kuroda
D · Fumikazu Sakurada
企画会社

**London International Festival
of Theatre**

England 1986

Pentagram Design Ltd.

AD · John McConnell

D · John McConnell, Leigh Brownsword

ロンドン国際演劇フェスティバル

Miragen

Biotechnology research and
development company

USA 1988

Mitsunaga[2]

AD · Tracy Mitsunaga

D · Tracy Mitsunaga, Alice Mitsunaga

C · Mentus, Inc.

バイオテクノロジー・リサーチ・開発会社

VIA

French furniture institute

France 1984

Grapus

AD, D, A · Grapus

フランス家具研究所

Computer Control Services Ltd.

Computer company subsidiary

England 1987/88

Liz James Design Associates

AD · Liz James

D · Liz James, Vicky Gornall

A · Brian Grimwood

コンピュータ会社の子会社

Bourque Pierre & Fils
Housing developer
Canada 1986
Furman Graphic Design
AD, D · Aviva Furman
住宅開発会社

Technology Response
High technology consultants
England 1986
The Partners (Design Consultants) Ltd.
AD · Aziz Cami
D · James Beveridge
A · Gary Powell
ハイテク・コンサルタント会社

Executive Systems, Inc.
Computer software company
USA 1987
Gormley/Takei, Inc.
AD, D, A · Koji Takei
コンピュータ・ソフト会社

Charlene & Robert Burningham
Designers/Weavers
USA 1986
Ikola Designs
AD, D · Gale William Ikola
テキスタイルデザイナー

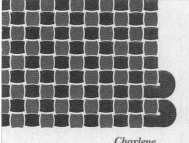

Duda Design
Design firm
USA 1987
Arnold Schwartzman Productions, Inc.
AD, D · Arnold Schwartzman
デザイン・スタジオ

Southern Printing
Printing company
Australia 1987
Flett Henderson & Arnold
AD · Richard Henderson
D, A · Flett Henderson & Arnold
印刷会社

160

Swid Powell
Tableware design
USA 1986
Skolos Wedell + Raynor, Inc.
AD, D · Nancy Skolos
食器デザイン

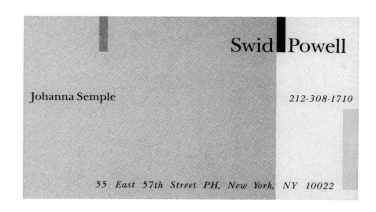

Conrad Theodore Partnership
Architects
Australia 1988
Emery Vincent Associates
AD, D, A · Emery Vincent Associates
建築設計事務所

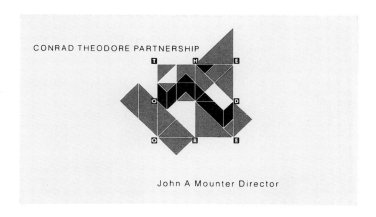

D. Ken Yoshikawa, DDS, MS
Dentist
USA 1986
The Design Office of Wong & Yeo
AD, D, A · Valerie Wong
歯科医師

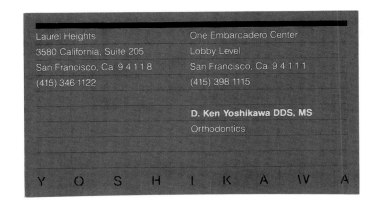

Stonesmith
Travel agency
Canada 1986
Neville Smith Graphic Design
AD, D, A · Neville Smith
旅行会社

Olympic Spirit Team
USA 1982
Arnold Schwartzman Productions, Inc.
AD, D · Arnold Schwartzman
C · Los Angeles Olympic Organizing
  Committee
ロサンゼルス五輪組織委員会

Karl/Piaia
Consulting architects
USA 1985
The Design Office of Wong & Yeo
AD, D, A · Valerie Wong
建築コンサルタント会社

Beach Front
Seaside restaurant
Australia 1987
Flett Henderson & Arnold
AD · Richard Henderson
D, A · Flett Henderson & Arnold
レストラン

Musée Internationale Co., Ltd.
Retail store of designed goods
Japan 1988
Igarashi Studio
AD · Takenobu Igarashi
D · Ross McBride
デザイン商品販売店

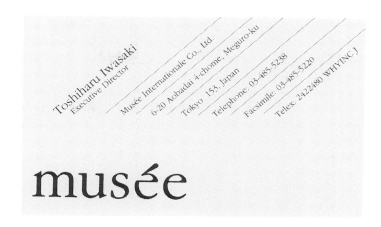

Traction Avenue
Fashion boutique
USA 1989
Ph.D
AD · Clive Piercy, Michael Hodgson
D · Clive Piercy
A · Ann Field
ファッション・ブティック

**Central Administration Office
Rotterdam**
Netherlands 1988
Vorm Vijf Grafisch Ontwerpteam GVN
AD, D · Bart de Groot
ロッテルダム市庁

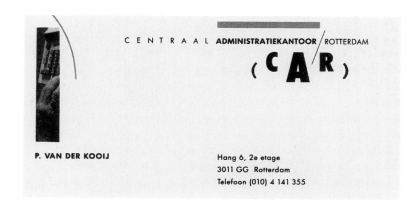

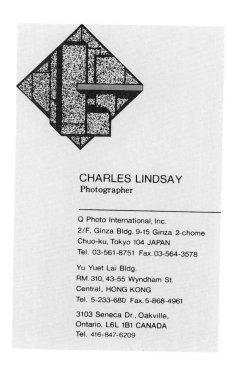

CHARLES LINDSAY
Photographer

Q Photo International, Inc.
2/F, Ginza Bldg. 9-15 Ginza 2-chome
Chuo-ku, Tokyo 104 JAPAN
Tel. 03-561-8751 Fax. 03-564-3578

Yu Yuet Lai Bldg.
RM. 310, 43-55 Wyndham St.
Central, HONG KONG
Tel. 5-233-680 Fax. 5-868-4961

3103 Seneca Dr., Oakville,
Ontario, L6L 1B1 CANADA
Tel. 416-847-6209

I do
Photo/Video studio
Hong Kong 1988
Kan Tai-keung Design & Associates Ltd.
AD, D · Eddy Yu
C · Simon So
写真/ビデオ・スタジオ

Charles Lindsay
Photographer
Canada 1988
Douglas Design Office
AD, D · Douglas Doolittle
写真家

Gary McCoy
Photographer
USA 1987
Summerford Design, Inc.
AD, D · Jack Summerford
A · Gary McCoy
写真家

M. Sokolsky
Photographer
USA 1970
Federico Design
AD, D · Gene Federico
写真家

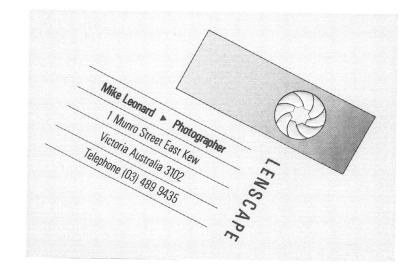

Lenscape
Photographer
Australia 1987
Cozzolino/Ellett Design D'Vision
AD · Philip Ellett
D, A · Rosanna DiRisio
C · Mike Leonard
写真家

Irongate Studios Ltd.
Photographer
England 1971
Trickett & Webb Ltd.
AD, D · Lynn Trickett, Brian Webb
A · John Summerhayes
写真家

Grapevine Caterers
Australia 1988
Condon Payne Terry Pty. Ltd.
AD · Clyde Terry
D, A · Stuart Wilson
ケイタリング会社

Harp Lager
Brewery
England 1987
Michael Peters Group PLC
AD · Glenn Tutssel
D · Paul Browton
ビール会社

Fox & Henderson's
Cafe-bar
England 1988
Design House Consultants Ltd.
AD, D · Kate Fishenden
A · Jonathan Mercer
C · Thistle Hotels Ltd.
カフェ・バー

Snoqualmie
Winery
USA 1985
Rick Eiber Design
AD, D · Rick Eiber
ワイン会社

Jubilee Yacht Charters
Cruise chartering company
USA 1984
Jack Hough Associates
AD · Jack Hough
D · Henry Goerke
A · Karl Maruyama
ヨット・チャーター会社

Gasthof Bahnhof
Restaurant
Switzerland 1982
BBV
AD, D · Michael Baviera
レストラン

NDC Graphics
Planning/Design team
Japan 1987
NDC Graphics
AD · Kenzo Nakagawa
D · Kenzo Nakagawa, Hiroyasu Nobuyama
デザイン会社のデザイン企画/制作室

株式会社日本デザインセンター
〒104 東京都中央区銀座1-13-13中央大和ビル
電話03-567-3231(代表)

総合グラフィックス研究室 室長
中川 憲造
Nakagawa kenzo

Posh Fusion Institute, Inc.
Corporate identity consultants
Japan 1987
Tokiyoshi Tsubouchi
AD, D · Tokiyoshi Tsubouchi
C. I.コンサルタント会社

株式会社 ポッシュ総合研究所

POSh

代表取締役社長
青山孝雄

本社：名古屋市中区栄2-9-9 表示灯ビル 〒460
TEL：052-202-1915 FAX：052-202-1925
東京オフィス： 東京都港区南青山5-12-12
ポッシュ表示灯ビル 〒107 TEL：03-797-4712

Mothers Deluxe Inc.
Advertising consultants
Japan 1988
Asaba Design Co., Ltd.
AD · Katsumi Asaba
D · Teruo Kataoka
広告コンサルタント会社

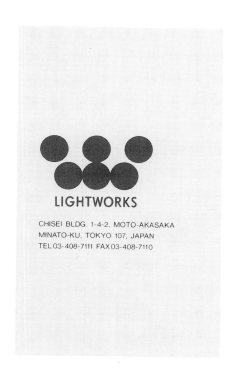

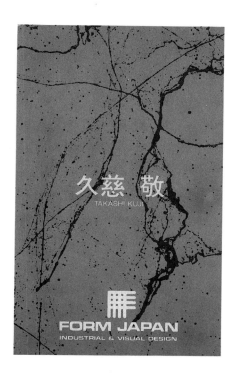

Lightworks
Lighting design company
Japan 1988
Kamijyo Studio
AD · Takahisa Kamijyo
D · Yuzo Fujiwara
照明デザイン会社

Form Japan
Industrial design firm
Japan 1987
See Saw
AD, D, A · Osamu Furumura
インダストリアルデザイン会社

Doshitemo Makinochanbaraga Mitainda Co.
Film production company
Japan 1985
K-Two Co., Ltd.
AD · Keisuke Nagatomo
D · Masayuki Takahashi
A · Seitaro Kuroda
映画製作会社

450 Summer Street
Boston MA
02210

617   350 4090

Robert F Daylor PE PLS
Principal

R W Electronics, Inc.
Computer components
USA 1984
Laughlin/Winkler
AD, D · Mark Laughlin, Ellen Winkler
コンピュータ部品会社

The BSC Group
Environmental engineers
USA 1987
Laughlin/Winkler
AD, D · Mark Laughlin, Ellen Winkler
環境エンジニアリング会社

1445 Main Street
Tewksbury/MA 01876

617 851 3113

Telex 820018
Facs 617 851 3728

R W Electronics, Inc

Peter Le Saffre
President

Technology Venture Investors
Venture capital firm
USA 1987
Gillian/Craig Associates
AD · Craig Sheumaker
D · Marc Kundmann
投資会社

Impex Diamond Corporation
USA 1984
Graphic Communication Concepts
AD, D · Sudarshan Dheer
A · Narendra Vaidya
ダイヤモンド販売会社

V & A Enterprises Ltd.
Retail operation
England 1988
Michael Peters Group PLC
AD · Glenn Tutssel
D · Wendy Metson
美術館の販売店経営

Casa Vogue
Beauty care services
Canada 1988
Lawrence Finn and Associates Ltd.
AD, A · Lawrence Finn
D · Amanda Finn
美容サービス会社

Danilee Pty. Ltd.
Human resource consultants
Australia 1988
Raymond Bennett Design Associates
AD · Raymond Bennett
D · Eden Cariwright
人材コンサルタント会社

Lorin Enterprises
Importers/Exporters
Canada 1986
Rushton, Green and Grossutti Inc.
AD · Keith Rushton
D · Maureen Nishikawa
貿易会社

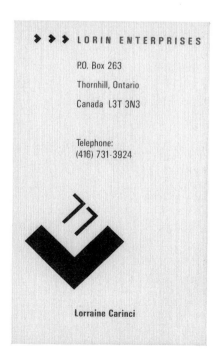

Bosscher, Dekker & van Heesen
Juridical planning advisers
Netherlands 1988
Vorm Vijf Grafisch Ontwerpteam GVN
AD, D · Bart de Groot
法律アドバイザー

Mrs. BOSSCHER, DEKKER & VAN HEESEN
Juridisch Planologische Adviseurs

Groothandelsgebouw C5
Weena 723
Postbus 29059
3001 GB Rotterdam
Telefoon (010)4045668
Telefax (010)4045669

Uilenburg 12
Postbus 472
5201 AL 's-Hertogenbosch
Telefoon (073)147837
Telefax (073)143953

mr J.W. van Heesen

Henri Meschonnic
France 1986
Catherine Zask
AD, D, A · Catherine Zask
業種不明

HENRI MESCHONNIC

90 QUAI AUGUSTE PRÉVOST
77500 CHELLES · FRANCE
TÉL. (1) 60 08 91 35

Dolphin bv
Software systems
Netherlands 1988
Maarten Vijgenboom Design
AD, D, A · Maarten Vijgenboom
ソフトウエア・システム会社

Helburn + Hoyt
Partners who operate independently
selling artifacts
USA 1986
Gina Federico Graphic Design
AD, D · Gina Federico
物品販売業

Owen & Robin Pilon
Farm
Australia 1988
Raymond Lee & Associates Ltd.
AD, D · Raymond Lee
A · Winsome Lee
農場

Cumulus Systems Ltd.
Systems software company
England 1988
The Partners (Design Consultants) Ltd.
AD · David Stuart
D · Peter Carrow
システム・ソフトウエア会社

Warehouse Gallery
Nautical gallery
England 1986
Julia Alldridge Associates
AD, D · Julia Alldridge
A · Alan Jones
C · Jon Bannenberg
海洋ギャラリー

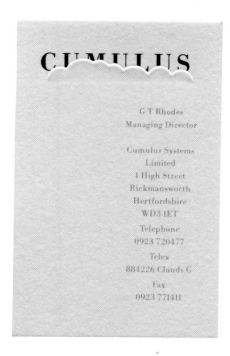

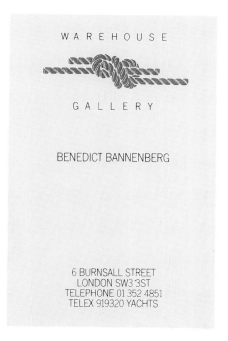

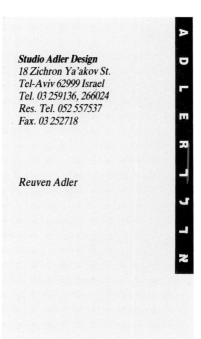

Richmond Medical/Dental Centre
Canada 1987
Eskind Waddell
AD · Roslyn Eskind
D · Christopher Campbell
C · Dr. Sidney Zucker
歯科医療センター

Studio Adler
Graphic design studio
Israel 1988
Studio Adler
AD · Reuven Adler
D · Ayelet Rubin
グラフィックデザイン・スタジオ

Studio Adler
Graphic design studio
Israel 1988
Studio Adler
AD · Reuven Adler
D · Ayelet Rubin
グラフィックデザイン・スタジオ

Charles Letts Ltd.
Publisher of diaries and addressbooks
England 1985
W M de Majo Associates
A · W M de Majo
D · W M de Majo MBA FCSD
C · Charles Letts & Co., Ltd.
日記帳/住所録出版社

Charles Letts Books Ltd
77 Borough Road
London SE1 1DW
Telephone 01-407 8891

Ray Pring
Book Representative

39 Shepherd Leaze
Wotton-under-Edge
Gloucestershire
Telephone 045-385 3435

D.F. Denby, FCIS
Director

Charles Letts & Co Ltd,
Diary House, 77 Borough Road
London SE1 1DW
Telephone: 01-407 8891
Telex: 884498 Letts G

J. M. Letts
Managing Director

Letts Andersons Ltd
Thornybank Industrial Estate
Dalkeith
Midlothian, EH22 2NE
Telephone 031-663 1971

CPT World Headquarters
Design firm
Australia 1988
Condon Payne Terry Pty. Ltd.
AD, D, A · CPT
C · CPT
デザイン会社

Ann Bohlen Graphic Development Representative
Artists' representative
USA 1980
Milton Glaser, Inc.
AD, D, A · Milton Glaser
C · Ann Bohlen, Milton Glaser Inc.
アーティストの権利交渉代理業

Helen & Gene Federico
Graphic designers
USA 1970
Federico Design
AD, D · Gene Federico
グラフィックデザイナー

Bennett/Harty Corporate Communications

Financial and corporate communications consultants

Australia 1986

Raymond Bennett Design Associates

AD, D · Raymond Bennett

金融/企業コンサルタント会社

Dieter Blum

Photographer

West Germany 1986

Stankowski + Duschek

AD, D · Stankowski + Duschek

写真家

Koniszczer Sapoznik Graphic Designers

Argentina 1988

Koniszczer Sapoznik Graphic Designers

AD, D · Marcelo Sapoznik,
Gustavo Koniszczer

グラフィックデザイン・スタジオ

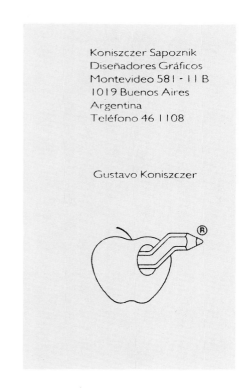

Ikola Designs
Graphic designer
USA 1974
Ikola Designs
AD, D · Gale William Ikola
グラフィックデザイナー

Gregory Thomas Associates
Design consultants
USA 1988
Gregory Thomas Associates
AD, D · Gregory Thomas
デザイン・コンサルタント会社

**Gregory Thomas
Associates**

**Design
Consultants**

2238½ Purdue Avenue
Los Angeles, California
90064

Telephone:
213 479.8477

FAX:
213 473.0904

Gregory Thomas
President

Laura A. Lazzeretti
Graphic designer
Argentina 1983
Estudio Hache
AD, D · Laura A. Lazzeretti
グラフィックデザイナー

Laura A. Lazzeretti
Diseño Gráfico
11 de Septiembre 1471
1426 Capital Federal
783-1014
782-3725

Pat Hansen Design
Graphic design firm
USA 1987
Pat Hansen Design
AD · Pat Hansen
D · Pat Hansen, Jesse Doquilo
グラフィックデザイン会社

Pat Hansen, President

Pat Hansen Design
618 Second Ave., Suite 1080
Seattle, Washington 98104
Telephone 206.467.9959

Richard Moore Associates
Design firm
USA 1972
Richard Moore Associates
AD, D · Richard Moore
デザイン会社

Richard Moore Associates

Richard Moore

21 Bond Street   New York, New York 10012
Telephone 212 673-4965

CaterWong
Design consultants
England 1984
CaterWong
AD, D · Phil Carter, Phil Wong
デザイン・コンサルタント会社

CARTER WONG
7 ROYALTY STUDIOS, 105 LANCASTER ROAD, LONDON W11 QF
TELEPHONE 01-221 5753

Design Consultants. Design Consultants.
PHILIP CARTER

Ski Train
Railroad service for skiers
USA 1974
David Leigh
AD, D, A · David Leigh
スキー客のための鉄道輸送サービス

Barrett C. Leete
President

SKI TRAIN

Dean Hill Road, Killington, Vermont 05751
(802) 422-3558
New York Office: (212) 371-1815

Masaross
Personal business card
Japan 1988
Ross McBride
AD, D, A · Ross McBride
個人用名刺

MASAS
水口政美
Masami Mizuguchi
ROSS

Technolease
Computer leasing
Canada 1984
Rushton, Green and Grossutti Inc.
AD · Rushton, Green and Grossutti Inc.
D · Mercello Grossutti
コンピュータ・リース会社

Technolease

Toronto
6303 Airport Rd.,
Suite 300,
Mississauga, Ontario
Canada L4V 1R8
(416) 677-3961

Walt Disney Concert Hall Committee
USA 1988
Sussman/Prejza + Co.
AD · Deborah Sussman
D · Felice Matarè
C · Music Center of Los Angeles County
コンサート・ホール委員会

Walt Disney Concert Hall Committee

Frederick M. Nicholas
Chairman

9300 wilshire
boulevard #200
beverly hills
california 90212
213 271-5176

Nottoway Plantation Home
USA 1983
Louis Nelson Associates Inc.
AD · Louis Nelson
D · L. Nelson, P. Scavuzzo
農場経営

Technichem
Engineering company
USA 1985
Noreen Rei Fukumori
AD, D · Noreen Rei Fukumori
C · Mark NG
エンジニアリング会社

Press Archives
Newspaper archive
England 1988
Trickett & Webb Ltd.
AD · Lynn Trickett, Brian Webb
D · Flona Skelsey
C · Robert Heron
新聞編集プロダクション

Cudmen Pty. Ltd.
Importers
Australia 1987
Raymond Bennett Design Associates
AD · Raymond Bennett
D · Victoria McNeill
輸入会社

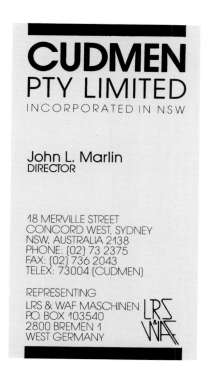

Magis
Editor
France 1986
Grapus
AD, D, A · Grapus
編集者

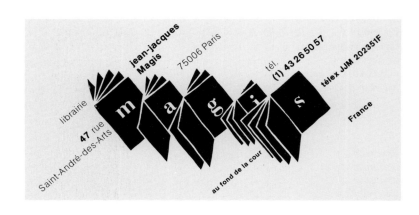

Sasha Pak
Manufacturers of sachet packs
Australia 1988
The Corporate Personality
AD, D · Ray A. Storey
におい袋製造会社

Chartwell I.R.M. Inc.
Computer planning & programming
company
Canada 1987
Kramer Design Associates Ltd.
AD · Burton Kramer
D · Burton Kramer, Jeremy Kramer
A · Kramer Design Associates Ltd.
コンピュータ・プログラミング会社

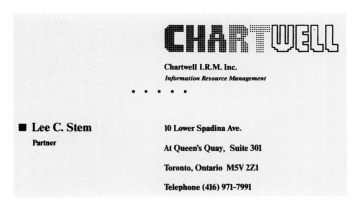

New Directions
Career counseling service
USA 1985
Manigault Designs
AD, D, A · Richard K. Manigault
カウンセリング会社

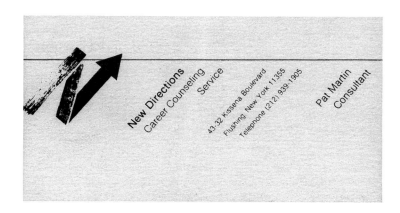

Ho Ming for Hair
Hair salon
USA 1988
M Design
AD, D · Glenn Mitsui, Jesse Doquilo
A · Glenn Mitsui
美容院

Sue Brown
Writer
England 1988
Julia Alldridge Associates
AD, D, A · Julia Alldridge
執筆家

Surya Roadlines
India 1980
Majeed A. A.
AD, D, A · Majeed A. A.
業種不明

1415 Western Ave. Suite 400 ▪

Seattle, Washington 98101 206.621.8704

Ho Man Woo
Designer

!
SUE BROWN
24 Hazlitt Road / London W14 0JY
Telephone 01 603 8804
Fax 01 602 1724
;

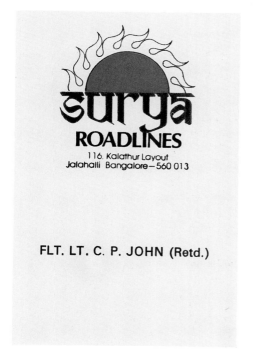

FLT. LT. C. P. JOHN (Retd.)

The Arbour
Qualicare hospital
USA 1982
Louis Nelson Associates Inc.
AD · Louis Nelson
D · L. Nelson, R. Jorgenson
病院

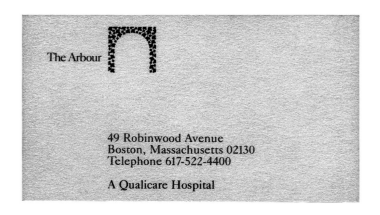

Coming Home Hospice
Home for the terminally ill
USA 1985
The design Office of Wong & Yeo
AD, D, A · Hock Wah Yeo
病気治療施設

River West Medical Center
USA 1983
Louis Nelson Associates Inc.
AD · Louis Nelson
D · L. Nelson, P. Scavuzzo
医療センター

O'Connor Company
Construction company
USA 1980
Witherspoon Design
AD, D · Randy Lynn Witherspoon
建設会社

Whitaker Construction Corporation
USA 1986
Skolos Wedell + Raynor, Inc.
AD, D · Cheryl Lilley
建設会社

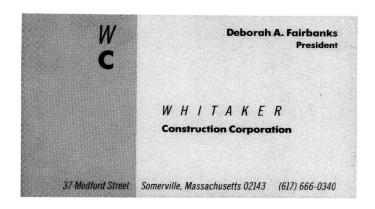

Esti · Mate
Builders
Australia 1986
Chris Payne Pty. Ltd.
AD, D, A · Chris Payne
建築会社

Carol Delong
Mime
USA 1981
Crosby Associates Inc.
AD, D · Bart Crosby
マイム

E & C Romanin
Paving contractors
Australia 1978
Mimmo Cozzolino Design
AD, D · Mimmo Cozzolino
A · Megan Williams
舗装会社

Hermann Bähler
Carpenter firm
Switzerland 1968
BBV
AD, D · Michael Baviera
建築会社

The Pleasure is All Mime, **Carol DeLong**, Mime

1358 W. Greenleaf, Chicago 60626 312.274.3534

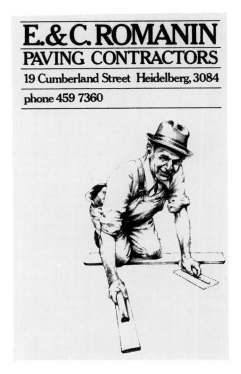

E.&C. ROMANIN
PAVING CONTRACTORS
19 Cumberland Street Heidelberg, 3084

phone 459 7360

Hermann Bähler
dipl. Schreinermeister
Möbelwerkstätte Innenausbau
4803 Vordemwald
Telefon 062 51 61 15

Raumgestaltung
Innenausbau
Gaststätten
Läden, Büros, Privat
Einzelmöbel
Aussteuern
Bettinhalte

Yajna Knitwear
Clothing designer
USA 1987
Ph.D
AD, D · Michael Hodgson
C · Koushna Navabi
衣料デザイナー

Sportsschool Kees Tempel
Sports school
Netherlands 1987
Vorm Vijf Grafisch Ontwerpteam GVN
AD, D · Eric van Casteren
スポーツ・スクール

Hans Groenwold Film-produktieleiding
Film production company
Netherlands 1987
Frans Lieshout
AD, D · Frans Lieshout
映画製作会社

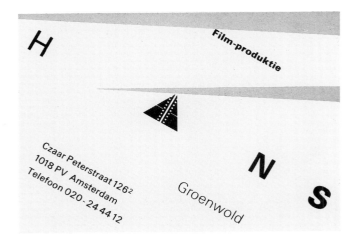

Integre Corporation
Computer systems development company
Japan 1989
Katsuichi Ito Design Office
AD, D · Katsuichi Ito
コンピュータ・システム開発会社

Dan + Aoshima Associates
Architectural firm
Japan 1986
Minoru Niijima Design Studio
AD, D · Minoru Niijima
建築設計会社

Ralph Selby and Associates
Design firm
England 1988
Julia Alldridge Associates
AD, D · Julia Alldridge
A · Sid Madge
デザイン会社

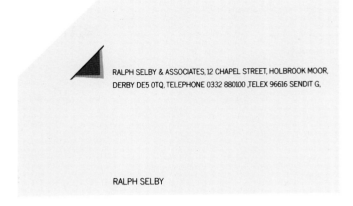

RALPH SELBY & ASSOCIATES, 12 CHAPEL STREET, HOLBROOK MOOR, DERBY DE5 0TQ, TELEPHONE 0332 880100 ,TELEX 96616 SENDIT G,

RALPH SELBY

Natper Corporation
Hotels and restaurants
USA 1986
Girish Patel Design Studio
AD, D, A · Girish Patel
ホテル/レストラン

Natpar Corporation

Nitin Kashiparekh, President

2820 Chamblee Tucker Road
Atlanta, Georgia 30341
Telephone: 404-458-7034

Terra Communication, Inc.
Consulting firm in engineering
USA 1985
Girish Patel Design Studio
AD, D, A · Girish Patel
エンジニアリング・コンサルタント会社

TerraCom

John E. Rectenwald
President

Terra Communications, Inc.
855 Mt. Vernon, N.E.
Suite 225
Atlanta, Georgia 30328
404-252-5200

Lesley Macmillan
Interior designer
Canada 1983
Neville Smith Graphic Design
AD, D, A · Neville Smith
インテリアデザイナー

Karen Alexander
Clothing manufacturer
USA 1985
Carron Design
AD, D · Ross Carron
衣料メーカー

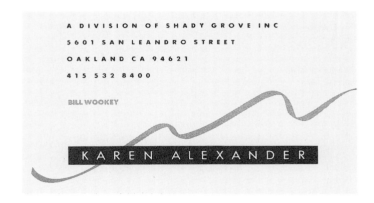

Fashion Transport
Transporter of clothes
Netherlands 1986
Maarten Vijgenboom Design
AD, D, A · Maarten Vijgenboom
衣料品輸送会社

Pamela Bruce Associates
Interior design firm
USA 1986
Skolos Wedell + Raynor, Inc.
AD, D · Cheryl Lilley
インテリアデザイン会社

Mosaic Theater
USA 1988
Paul Davis Studio
AD · Paul Davis
D · Jose Conde
劇場

The International Design Group
Interior design office
Canada 1986
Rushton, Green and Grossutti Inc.
AD · Keith Rushton
D · Gildo Martino, Kirsti Ronback
インテリアデザイン・オフィス

Art Circulation
Intermediary of modern art
Netherlands 1987
Maarten Vijgenboom Design
AD, D, A · Maarten Vijgenboom
美術品販売仲介業

Julie Brand
Artist
Australia 1981
Cozzolino Hughes
AD, D · Mimmo Cozzolino
A · David Hughes
アーティスト

Barbara DeWitt
Artists representative
USA 1988
Ph.D
AD, D · Clive Piercy, Michael Hodgson
アーティストの権利交渉代理人

Group Ma
Choreographic center
France 1987
Catherine Zask
AD, D, A · Catherine Zask
舞踊研究所

Ceramics/Raku
Ceramic artist
USA 1986
Noreen Rei Fukumori
AD, D · Noreen Rei Fukumori
C · Dina Angel-Wing
陶芸家

Bad Mothers
Artists who are mothers
Australia 1987
Ned Culic Design Pty. Ltd.
AD, D · Ned Culic
ママさんアーティスト・グループ

Susana Klik
Designer
Spain 1984
Medina Design
AD, D · Fernando Medina
デザイナー

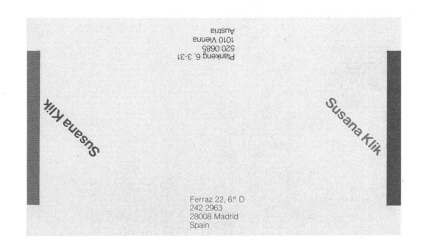

Typhoon Pictures Ltd.
Hong Kong 1988
Graphic Communication Ltd.
AD, D · Henry Steiner
A · Po, Hing Ming
映画会社

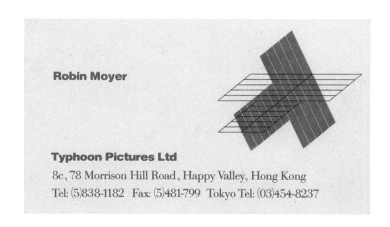

Bittman Vammen Taylor
Architects
USA 1986
Pat Hansen Design
AD · Pat Hansen
D · Pat Hansen, Paula Richards
建築設計事務所

Lithographix, Inc.
811 North Highland
Los Angeles, Calif. 90038
213 : 462-7236

Ian and Felicity Baker

2 IRVING ROAD

TOORAK VIC 3142

AUSTRALIA

PHONE (03) 20 6201

MESSAGES (03) 690 4522

7 rue Sainte Anne 75001 Paris tél (1) 42 97 56 22

ENFANT D'ABORD

yvonne Quilès rédactrice en chef adjointe

Lithographix, Inc.
Printing company
USA 1972
The Weller Institute for the Cure of
Design, Inc.
AD, D · Don Weller
A · Dan Hanrahan
印刷会社

Fresh Flicks
TV/Film production company
Australia 1988
Condon Payne Terry Pty. Ltd.
AD · CPT
D · Clyde Terry
A · Stu-art Wilson
C · Ian Baker
テレビ/映画製作会社

Enfant D'abord
Magazine
France 1986
Grapus
AD, D, A · Grapus
雑誌

Falcon Børsanalyser a.s
Finance analysis
Norway 1986/87
Enzo Finger
AD, D · Enzo Finger
金融アナリスト会社

Pianocraft
Grand piano restoration and rentals
Canada 1986
Neville Smith Graphic Design
AD, D, A · Neville Smith
ピアノの修復/レンタル会社

Gary Gladstone
Design firm
USA 1987
Milton Glaser, Inc.
AD, D, A · Milton Glaser
デザイン会社

Jonco Pty. Ltd.
Builders
Australia 1988
Fast Proof Commercial Printers
AD, D, A · Veronica Tasnadi
C · Jon Ingall
建築会社

Digital Systems International
High technology company
USA 1988
Tim Girvin Design
AD, D · Tim Girvin
D · Stephen Pannoe
コンピュータ・システム開発会社

Stane Gregorc
Painter for industrial products
Yugoslavia 1986
Studio KROG
AD, D · Edi Berk
製品塗装業

Trading Places Pty. Ltd.
Australia 1987
Sussman/Prejza + Co.
AD · Deborah Sussman
D · Corky Retson
貿易会社

Artfile/BCE Systems Inc.
USA 1986
David Curry Design Inc.
AD, D · David Curry
業種不明

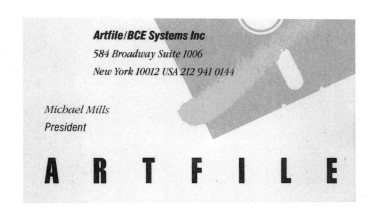

GEM International Co., Ltd.
Design consultants
Japan 1986
Igarashi Studio
AD · Takenobu Igarashi
D · Yukimi Sasago
デザイン・コンサルタント会社

Widgery Silk Architects
Architectural firm
USA 1984
Rick Eiber Design
AD, D · Rick Eiber
建築設計会社

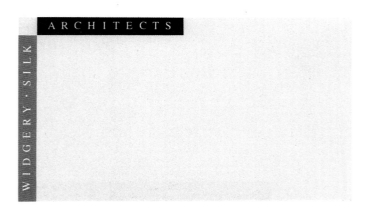

Walker Interactive Systems
Premium software company
USA 1988
Gillian/Craig Associates
AD · Gillian Smith
D · Judi Muller
プレミアム・ソフトウェア会社

CC Soft Drinks
Beverage company
England 1985
Michael Peters Group PLC
AD · Glenn Tutssel
D · Paul Browton
清涼飲料会社

Nutter Consulting Services
Employment consultants
USA 1989
Zender + Associates, Inc.
AD, D, A · Darla Haven Taylor
雇用コンサルタント会社

ACF Grew Inc.
Boat manufacturer
Canada 1988
Raymond Lee & Associates Ltd.
AD, D · Raymond Lee
A · Derek Chung Tiam Fook
ボート製造会社

Janez Jureš
Yugoslavia 1986
Studio KROG
AD, D · Edi Berk
A · Zvone Kosovelj
業種不明

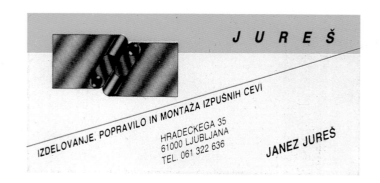

Essential Software
Computer software company
Australia 1988
Raymond Bennett Design Associates
AD · Raymond Bennett
D · Victoria McNeill
コンピュータ・ソフト会社

Beth Brosseau
Writing and consulting
USA 1987
Pat Hansen Design
AD · Pat Hansen
D · Pat Hansen, Paula Richards
執筆業/コンサルタント業

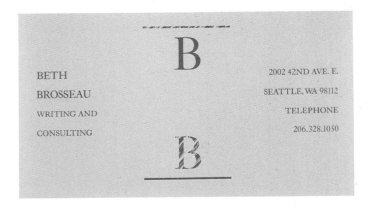

Pegasus Print & Display Ltd.
England 1987
KB Design
AD · Karen Blincoe
D · Karen Blincoe, Richard Fisher Smith
A · Richard Fisher Smith
印刷/ディスプレー会社

Sancho Design
Graphic designer
USA 1989
Sancho Design
AD, D · Sancho
グラフィックデザイナー

Peter Walberg Design
Design firm
USA 1989
Peter Walberg Design
AD, D · peter Walberg
デザイン会社

Anni & Bent Knudsen
Graphic designer
Denmark 1958
Anni & Bent Knudsen
AD, D, A · Bent Knudsen
グラフィックデザイナー

SANCHO DESIGN

100 Mercer Street
Seattle, WA 98109
Phone 206.285.1642

Sancho
Designer & Principal

Peter Walberg **Design** 213.578.7125

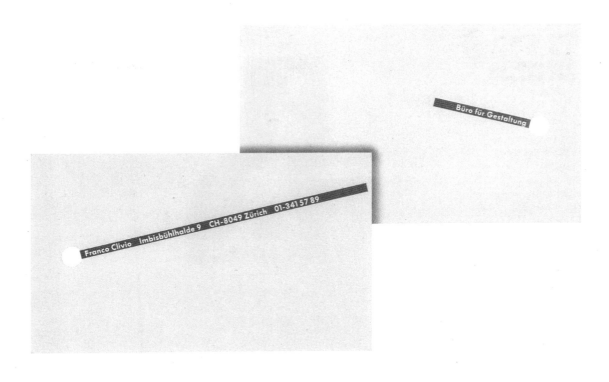

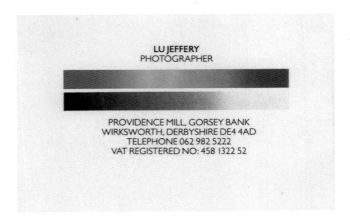

Franco Clivio
Industrial designer
Switzerland 1988
Franco Clivio
AD, D, A · Franco Clivio
インダストリアルデザイナー

Lu Jeffery
Photographer
England 1988
Julia Alldridge Associates
AD, D · Julia Alldridge
写真家

Gillian B.
Women's clothing store
USA 1987
Milton Glaser, Inc.
AD, D, A · Milton Glaser
婦人衣料品店

Wave Restaurant & Bar
Restaurant and Bar
USA 1985
Vigon Seireeni
AD, D, A · Vigon Seireeni
レストラン/バー

MusiCum Laude
Music production company
USA 1985
The Weller Institute for the Cure of
Design, Inc.
AD, D, A · Don Weller
音楽プロダクション

Judy Collins
USA 1982
Louis Nelson Associates Inc.
AD · Louis Nelson
D · L. Nelson, D. O'Keefe
C · Rocky Mountain Productions
プロダクション

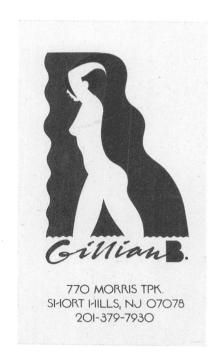

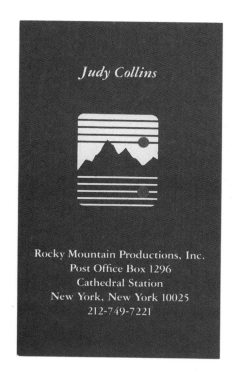

Decoustics
Manufacturer of interior acoustical
paneling
Canada 1986
Kramer Design Associates Ltd.
AD · Burton Kramer
D · Burton Kramer, J.P. Veilleux
A · Kramer Design Associates Ltd.
インテリア音響パネル会社

65 Disco Road
Etobicoke, Ontario
Canada M9W 1M2

Tel. (416) 675-3983
Telex 06-989323
FAX (416) 675-5546

decoustics decousti
decoustics
decoustics

Roy A. Hintsa
President

Maxon Systems Inc.
Importer of electronic parts
USA 1985
Gillian/Craig Associates
AD, D · Craig Sheumaker
電子部品輸入会社

maxon

MAXON SYSTEMS, INC.
130 KNOWLES DRIVE
LOS GATOS, CA 95030
(408)370-7722
FAX # (408)370-7131

JAMES DOYLE

TransCan Greetings
Distributor of paper goods
Canada 1987
LaPine/O'Very
AD, D, A · Traci O'Very Covey
紙工品販売会社

TRANS CAN
GREETINGS

DAVE JOHNSON
SALES REPRESENTATIVE
(403)435-8767

Chantrey Vellacott
Accounting firm
England 1988
Lloyd Northover Ltd.
AD · Jim Northover
D · Anne Donaldson
経理会社

Coates Signco Pty. Ltd.
Sign manufacturer
Australia 1986
Annette Harcus Design
AD, D, A · Annette Harcus
看板会社

United Telecoms Pvt. Ltd.
India 1987
Graphic Communication Concepts
AD, D · Sudarshan Dheer
A · Narendra Vaidya
通信会社

Different Tastes
Gourmet catering
USA 1981
Laughlin/Winkler
AD, D · Mark Laughlin, Ellen Winkler
C · Jack Milan
料理ケイタリング会社

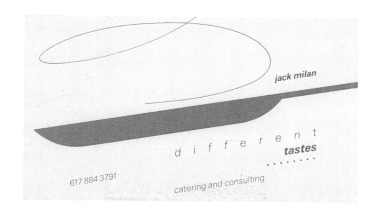

The Immune Response Corporation
Biotechnology company
USA 1988
Mitsunaga[2]
AD, D · Tracy Mitsunaga
C · Mentus, Inc.
バイオテクノロジー会社

Adele Freedman
Writer/Journalist on design
Canada 1988
Kramer Design Associates Ltd.
AD · Burton Kramer
D, A · Kramer Design Associates Ltd.
デザイン・ジャーナリスト

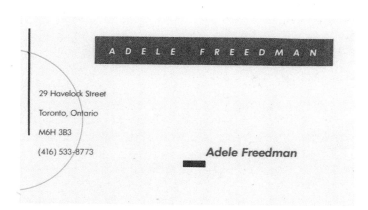

Thomas Associates
Graphic design firm
USA 1988
Gregory Thomas Associates
AD, D · Gregory Thomas
グラフィックデザイン会社

Ozubko Communication + Design Consultants
Graphic design firm
USA 1983
Ozubko Communication + Design Consultants
AD, D · Christopher Ozubko
グラフィックデザイン会社

Peter Grant
Graphic designer
USA 1988
Peter Grant
AD, D · Peter Grant
グラフィックデザイナー

Dimexon
Diamond importers and exporters
India 1985
Graphic Communication Concepts
AD, D · Sudarshan Dheer
A · Narendra Vaidya
ダイヤモンド輸出入会社

Pankaj K. Mehta

DIMEXON
Diamond Manufacturers Importers & Exporters

1202 Prasad Chambers,
Tata Road No. 2. Bombay-400 004.
Gram: "SHONINA"
Telex:011-5993 Phone:359956 369315

Notter Finegold + Alexander Inc.
Architectural firm
USA 1987
Laughlin/Winkler
AD, D · Mark Laughlin, Ellen Winkler
建築設計会社

Notter Finegold + Alexander Inc

Architects and
Preservation Planners

Karle S Packard, AIA

77 North Washington Street
Boston MA 02114 2193

617 227 9272

Gimnasio Irma Mogilevsky
Sports facilities
Argentina 1987
Daniel Higa, Carlos Venancio
Comunicación Visual
AD, D, A · Daniel Higa,
Carlos Venancio
スポーツ・センター

GIM
gimnasio
irma mogilevsky

Claudio Daiban
director

migueletes 868 · la imprenta
1426 buenos aires · argentina
tel. 772-5747|0294|1777
773-7098|3283

Ray Sābō
Architectural remodeling company
USA 1984
Zender + Associates, Inc.
AD, D, A · Priscilla A. W. Fisher
建築改修会社

AIDS Housing of Washington
A non-profit organization for persons
with AIDS
USA 1988
M Design
AD, D · Jesse Doquilo, Glenn Mitsui
A · Jesse Doquilo
エイズ救済団体

Chancery Corporate Support
Australia 1986
Rick Lambert Design Consultants
AD, D, A · Rick Lambert
経営コンサルタント会社

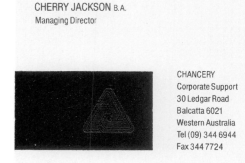

Hong Kong Designers Association
Hong Kong 1984
Kan Tai-keung Design & Associates Ltd.
AD · Kan Tai-keung
D · Freeman Lau
ホンコン・デザイナーズ協会

Susan Lynn Stegmuller
Commercial pilot
USA 1988
Vigon Seireeni
AD, D, A · Vigon Seireeni
商業飛行士

Fineline Studio
Artwork studio
England 1988
Trickett & Webb Ltd.
AD · Lynn Trickett, Brian Webb
D · Lynn Trickett, Brian Webb,
     Ashley Carter
A · David Mawford
版下制作スタジオ

ZB Inc.
Design firm
USA 1985
Weisz Yang Dunkelberger Inc.
AD · Larry Yang
D · Eric Nash
デザイン会社

Powers and Company Inc.
Architectural firm
USA 1984
Laughlin/Winkler
AD, D · Mark Laughlin, Ellen Winkler
建築設計会社

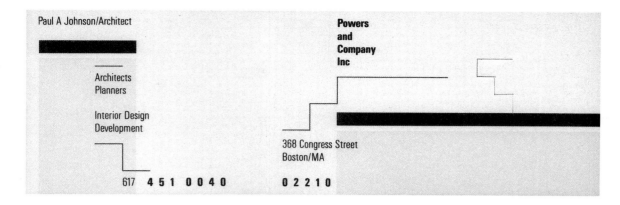

Quantum
Spain 1984
Medina Design
AD, D · Fernando Medina
業種不明

Ron C. Dunkley Architects
Australia 1988
Raymond Bennett Design Associates
AD · Raymond Bennett
D · Eden Cartwright
建築設計会社

Ofício
Office workshop of architects
Brazil 1985
Ao Lapis Studio (Animus Propaganda)
AD, D · Rique Nitzsche
A · Tuninho De Paula
建築事務所

Visconde Silva, 79/2.º
Tel.: (021) 286-8994
Botafogo/22.281
Rio de Janeiro

CARLOS EDUARDO DE LACERDA

Imagimax
Concept company
Canada 1986
Lawrence Finn and Associates Ltd.
AD, D · Amanda Finn
企画会社

Michael Wilkings

Imagimax Corporation
19 Isabella Street, Toronto, Canada M4Y 1M7
Telephone (416) 924-3300 Fax (416) 924-0774
Toronto · Los Angeles · Sydney

Animus Propaganda
Design consultants
Brazil 1987
Ao Lapis Studio (Animus Propaganda)
AD, D, A · Rique Nitzsche
デザイン・コンサルタント会社

Antônio Henrique Nitzsche

Animus Propaganda
Ladeira do Ascurra, 115-A
Cosme Velho/22241/Rio
Telefone: (021) 205-2777

Floristics
Florists
USA 1981
Manigault Designs
AD, D, A · Richard K. Manigault
花屋

Interfaith Caregivers Coalition, Inc.
USA 1985
Manigault Designs
AD, D, A · Richard K. Manigault
異宗派間交流団体

PBI Cambridge
International technological plant
breeding company
England 1988
Michael Peters Group PLC
AD · Glenn Tutssel
D · Tim Lehy
C · Unilever
品種改良技術開発会社

William Stout Architects
USA 1988
Tenazas Design
AD, D · Lucille Tenazas
建築設計事務所

William Stout Architect

804 Montgomery Street

San Francisco CA 94133

415 391.6808

W S | A

Dunkley & Company
Floral design group
England 1987
CarterWong
AD · Phil Carter, Phil Wong
D · Alison Tomlin
A · Thorogood Burgess
フラワーデザイン会社

DUNKLEY & COMPANY
THE CREATIVE FLORAL DESIGN GROUP

LYNN DUNKLEY
Director

28 ORMONDE ROAD EAST SHEEN LONDON SW14 7BG
TELEPHONE 01 878 8734 TELEX 312678 COPMUS G

Member of the Association of Conference Executives

Evangel Heights United Methodist Church
Religious organization
USA 1985
Ikola Designs
AD, D · Gale William Ikola
宗教団体

Come Share Christ

Larry L. Houseman, Pastor
114 North Ironwood Drive
South Bend, Indiana 46615

Evangel Heights
United Methodist Church
Church Office (219) 234-8379

Pamela Virgilio Design
67 Vestry Street
New York, NY 10013
USA
20

Pat Hansen Design
618 Second Avenue, Suite 1080
Seattle, WA 98104
USA
179. 194. 201

Pat Taylor Inc.
3540 S Street N.W.
Washington, D.C. 20007
USA
79

Paul Davis Studio
14 East 4th Street #504
New York, NY 10012
USA
113, 146, 191

Paul Rand Inc.
87 Good Hill Road
Weston, CT 06883
USA
57

Pesca *
23 East 22nd Street
New York, NY 10010
USA
102

Peter Grant
859 N McCadden Place #6
Hollywood, CA 90038
USA
208

Peter Walberg Design
825 Superba Avenue
Venice, CA 90291
USA
202

Playne Design
96 Fort Greene Place
Brooklyn, NY 11217
USA
101

Qris Yamashita
707 Robinson Street
Los Angeles, CA 90026
USA
52

Rick Eiber Design
4649 Sunnyside Ave. N. #242
Seattle, WA 98103
USA
33, 66, 95, 116, 128, 167, 199

Robert Miles Runyan & Associates
200 East Culver Boulevard
Playa del Rey, CA 90293
USA
69

Robert T. Wormald *
acti
Eight Farm Springs
Farmington, CT 06032
USA
44

Roberts Jones Associates, Inc. *
1550 East Meadowbrook
Phoenix, AZ 85014
USA
41

Rod Dyer Group Inc.
8360 Melrose Avenue
Los Angeles, CA 90069
USA
12, 13, 28, 29, 113, 114, 127

Ross McBride
1123 Perry HWY
Pittsburgh, PA 15237
USA
152, 180

Sancho Design
100 Mercer Street
Seattle, WA 98109
USA
52, 202

Saul Bass/Herb Yager & Associates
7039 Sunset Boulevard
Los Angeles, CA 90026
USA
67

Shimokochi/Reeves Design
6043 Hollywood Boulevard
Suite 203
Los Angeles, CA 90028
USA
15, 88, 92, 125, 135

Skolos Wedell + Raynor, Inc.
The Schrafft Center
529 Main Street
Charlestown, MA 02129
USA
30, 32, 34, 161, 185, 191

Society of Environmental Graphic Designers
47 Third Street
Cambridge, MA 012141
USA
44

Square One Preschool *
413 North 7th Avenue
Phoeniz, AZ 85007
USA
40

Steff Geissbuhler
60 Hollywood drive,
Hastings-on-Hudson
New York, NY 10706
USA
87, 131

Steven A. Heller
5808 Nagle Avenue
Van Nuys, CA 91401
USA
77

Steven V. Correia Design
P.O. Box 294
Topanga, CA 90290
USA
78

Summerford Design, Inc.
2706 Fairmount
Dallas, TX 75201
USA
105, 164

Sussman/Prejza & Company, Inc.
3960 Ince Boulevard
Culver City, CA 90230
USA
121, 151, 180, 198

Tandem Studios
324 South 400 West
Salt Lake City, UT 84101
USA
18

Tenazas Design
448 Bryant
San Francisco, CA 94107
USA
142, 215

Thane Roberts
1424 4th Street
Santa Monica, CA 90401
USA
55

The Appelbaum Company
176 Madison Avenue
New York, NY 10016
USA
93

The Design Office of Wong & Yeo
744 Union Street #1
San Francisco, CA 94133
USA
120, 126, 153, 161, 162, 184

The Nature Company *
10250 Santa Monica Boulevard
Los Angeles, CA 90067
USA
104

The Weller Institute for the Cure of Design, Inc.
P.O. Box 726, 1398 Aerie Drive
Park City, UT 84060
USA
111, 113, 195, 204

Tim Girvin Design, Inc.
911 Western Avenue
Suite 408
Seattle, WA 98104-1031
USA
32, 116, 149, 197

Timothy Hartford
6030 North Sheridan #1104
Chicago, IL 60660
USA
66, 123

Triad.
901 E Street
San Rafael, CA 94901
USA
74

UCI, Inc./Urano Communication International
1088 Bishop Street, Suite 1226
Honolulu, HI 96813
USA
16, 139

Vanderbeek & Chiow Advertising
130 S. Bemiston Avenue
St. Louis, MO 63105
USA
110, 140

Vanderbyl Design
539 Bryant Street
San Francisco, CA 94107
USA
119

Verbum (Computer Journal) *
4620 Panorama Drive
La Mesa, CA 92041
USA
103

Vigon Seireeni
708 W Orange Grove Avenue
Los Angeles, CA 90036
USA
134, 204, 211

Vita/Design
120 Belgrave Avenue
San Francisco, CA 94117
USA
110

Wayne Hunt Design, Inc.
87 North Raymond Avenue
Suite 215
Pasadena CA 91108-3996
USA
59

Weisz Yang Dunkelberger Inc.
61 Wilton Road
Westport, CT 06880
USA
118, 211

Will Gillis / Wordsmith *
1440 North Gardner #206
Los Angeles, CA 90046
USA
70

Witherspoon Design
1844 West 5th Avenue
Columbus, OH 43212
USA
185

Woody Pirtle
Pentagram Design Services Inc.
212 Fifth Avenue
New York, NY 10010
USA
79, 104

Yashi Okita Design
87 Stillman
San Francisco, CA 94107
USA
56

Zender + Associates, Inc.
2311 Park Avenue
Cincinnati, OH 45206
USA
64, 200, 210

Ziff Salisbury Design *
The Granada Bldg.
672 South Lafayette Park #28
Los Angeles, CA 90057
USA
117

Zuzana Licko Design
2431 Russell Street
Berkeley, CA 94705
USA
90

WEST GERMANY

Lang Art + Graphic-Design
Waldburgstrasse 17
Böblingen 7030
West Germany
65, 94, 108

Randolph Nolte Creative Consultants
Böhmersweg 24
2000 Hamburg 13
West Germany
13

Stankowski + Duschek
Lenbachstrasse 43
Stuttgart-1 7000
West Germany
177

Udo Schliemann
Gausstrasse 107
Stuttgart-1 7000
West Germany
144

WEST INDIES

Russel Halfhide Graphic Design
28 Angelina Street
St. James
Port of Spain, Trinidad
West Indies
139

YUGOSLAVIA

Katja Zelinka Skerlavaj
Linhartova 9
Ljubljana
Yugoslavia
97

Studio KROG
Krakovski nasip 22
61000 Ljubljana
Yugoslavia
127, 197, 200

* Complete information was not available by the time of publication.
＊ 連絡先が不明確、あるいは不明のもの。

BUSINESS CARDS
世界の名刺

1989 年 8 月 25 日　初版第 1 刷発行
1989 年 11 月 25 日　初版第 2 刷発行

定価　　　　　　　　10,300 円
編集　　　　　　　　五十嵐威暢 ⓒ
発行　　　　　　　　久世利郎
印刷・製本　　　　　凸版印刷株式会社
写真植字　　　　　　株式会社リンクス
　　　　　　　　　　三和写真工芸株式会社
発行所　　　　　　　株式会社グラフィック社
　　　　　　　　　　〒 102　東京都千代田区九段北 1-9-12
　　　　　　　　　　電話 03(263)4318　振替・東京 3-114345
　　　　　　　　　　落丁・乱丁はお取替え致します。

監修　　　　　　　　　　　五十嵐威暢
アートディレクション　　　五十嵐威暢
カバー・デザイン　　　　　五十嵐威暢
レイアウト　　　　　　　　白鳥佳容子
撮影　　　　　　　　　　　ナカサ＆パートナーズ
序文翻訳　　　　　　　　　ジェイ・W・トーマス
グラフィック社編集担当　　奥田政喜

ISBN4-7661-0531-1 C3070 P10300E